Contents

1. Preface

To be honest...

I never imagined I'd write a book about the future of law.

And definitely not one about AI.

Because I didn't grow up surrounded by courtrooms or legal textbooks.

I come from a different world —

a world of hotels, late check-ins, pressure to fill rooms, chasing targets, dealing with chaos, solving problems.

That world taught me a lot.

How to listen.

How to lead.

How to fix things fast without losing the human touch.

But most of all — it taught me this:

Technology changes everything.

It changes how people book a room.

How they ask for help.

How they make decisions — and how fast they expect answers.

And so, when I stepped into the legal field, with all its depth and history,

I couldn't ignore the feeling I had in my gut:

"We're still doing things the hard way."

I saw brilliant lawyers —

burnt out.

Smart firms —

losing clients because they couldn't respond quickly enough.

And legal services —

still too complicated, too expensive, too slow for the people who actually need them most.

That's when I knew:

Something had to change.

So no, this isn't a book about robots taking over courtrooms.

And it's not a tech manual filled with buzzwords.

This is a book about possibility.

About how we — the lawyers, the leaders, the students —

can adapt, evolve, and lead the legal profession into something better.

Faster, yes.

But also fairer.

Smarter — and more human.

If you're a lawyer wondering how to keep up —

This book is for you.

If you're a judge facing new kinds of evidence and tech-driven arguments —

This book is for you.

If you're a student trying to figure out where you fit in a changing industry —

This book is absolutely for you.

And if you're a managing partner or policy-maker,

Wondering how to balance tradition with transformation —

I wrote this book with you in mind too.

Inside, you'll find practical tools.

Real examples.

Honest thoughts.

A little frustration.

And a lot of hope.

You'll learn how AI can take the pressure off your team.

How marketing isn't just for selling — but for serving.

And how digital tools can make the law feel less like a maze,

and more like a service — the way it's meant to be.

I didn't write this because I have all the answers.

I wrote this because I know what it feels like

to step into a system

and see how much better it could be — if we just gave ourselves permission to rethink it.

I've seen what tech did for the hospitality industry.

And I know — without a doubt — it can do even more for law.

But we have to stop seeing AI as the enemy.

We have to stop thinking innovation means losing what makes us lawyers.

Because it doesn't.

So, here's my invitation:

Read this book with an open mind.

Challenge it.

Build on it.

Use it to start conversations with your team, your clients, your future self.

Because the future of law isn't written yet.

And maybe — just maybe — we get to write it together.

2. Introduction

Reflecting back in 2021, technology has truly advanced and changed the way we live our lives and interact with others so considerably that communicating, working, and going about our daily activities are entirely different from what they used to be. Through advancements like the evolution of AI, robotics, digital workspaces, and online collaborations, traditional industries have been transformed, and even social norms have changed.

The digital revolution has changed the way we interpret accessibility under the ADA, expanding it to include websites, mobile applications, and other digital platforms. The new focus on web accessibility standards, such as the Web Content Accessibility Guidelines (WCAG), has ensured that people with disabilities are the ones to benefit from such a framework. There is a multitude of features to consider companies and developers are asking to be implemented now, such as a screen reader compatible and keyboard navigable interface and an alternate text for images in order to make the digital product accessible and user-friendly.

Not only are enterprises obliged to abide by the law, but they also have a moral obligation to allow equal access to digital services to those who would otherwise be excluded from engagement in a digital world. Organizations that emphasize accessibility expose themselves to legal threats but concurrently tap into new marketing channels, offer better service to all customers, and build a more pluralistic society.

Throughout the digital age, innovations and research within the legal sector are at the centre of an ongoing evolution born mainly by mobile technology, the use of the cloud, the emergence of blockchain, AI as well as Natural Language Processing, etc. It has led to the more accessible and user-friendly mobile technology as legal services, and thus individuals can obtain legal aid anytime and anywhere. Furthermore, in the cloud computing era, the traditional paper-based systems of long-held and expensive document storage, as well as the exchange of information and interaction, are at the mercy of a revolutionary modification in that it is the 'cloud storage', which today has become synonymous with cheap and easier methods of the above. The first reason is that the major startups in this industry are becoming noticeably more open to the technology blockchain, the second is that this is a lot more secure of a transfer, and the third is that this is a smart contract, for instance, which is one of the simplest forms of transactions that businesses can do without an intermediary. AI and natural language processing have also helped lawyers and researchers in their studies, by providing them with effective tools to handle complex cases and guarantee accurate results in the legal domain.

The generation that has grown up with technology (Millennials and Generation Z) is mainly the cause of these technological advancements and this ever-changing digital landscape. They have also emerged as a potent group that can put pressure on law firms to innovate as they challenge traditional practices and exclude clients from simple issues. Thus, the legal sector needs to be aware of technology and make use of it skilling its employees in this regard in order to provide more preference to clients' needs. The use of technology will boost the efficiency, accessibility, and inclusivity of the legal industry, paving the way for social equity, and thus, the establishment of a more just society.

The progression toward becoming a part of the digital platforms and systems is evident in these initiatives. The transformation of processes, the enhancement of human capacities, and the involvement of digital technology are just a few of the methods by which businesses and legal practitioners can economize and make ethical and social changes better. The fast pace of advanced technology development can also hinder the poor access to legal services and the courts. The gap requires active engagement and assistance for resolution and advancement.

1. The Digital Divide

The digital divide is the distinction between those who have access to modern digital technology—including smartphones, laptops, and the internet—and those who do not. This divide can be observed in households, enterprises, and geographic regions. This divide can be influenced by a variety of factors, such as economic status, education level, geographic location, infrastructure availability, and digital literacy.

Access to technology is a critical component of the digital divide. This divide most affects those already marginalized within society—people living in poverty, minorities, women, and those who have low education and less access. Despite the popular idea that technology is spreading equally everywhere, a set of disadvantaged people and places remain on the wrong side of this global gap. In the legal profession, this technology access can contribute to inequality. Marginalized individuals who do not have representation, or who are represented by lawyers that do not have access to the best technology, can often get stuck in a system that neither provides justice nor affirms their human dignity merely to move forward in their lives. This phenomenon, whether digital or not, is detrimental to the soul of the rule of law.

The divide is heterogeneous and occurs because of the interaction of various factors. First, the digital divide can be associated with economic differences. Second, besides the economic divide, the digital divide can also be linked to educational disparities. Third, the availability of requisite infrastructure needed for internet access is a condition for bridging the divide. The digital divide is not restricted to just access to the physical infrastructure of technology. There is, additionally, a "second-level" digital divide involving those with access who do not make use of it. Fourth, the digital divide can have geographic components as areas in developed countries are more likely to get wired than peripheral areas in developing countries. Fifth, the principle of gender equality is an important factor as women lag behind men both in technology access and in technology use. Techniques for ending digital discrimination involve closing the infrastructure gaps as in the developed world, within nations, in terms of price and access; the development of more effective universal service strategies; telecommunications administrative reforms that endorse competition in urban and rural areas; rejuvenating the educational sphere; and increasing public involvement with the private sector for services and their media outlets.

My professional journey began in the vibrant world of hospitality, where I honed my skills in marketing and business development, ultimately achieving a remarkable 300% increase in revenue from hotel platforms within just few years. My experience in the hospitality sector taught me how to seamlessly blend traditional business practices with innovative digital solutions, successfully transforming transactional operations into robust digital platforms. It was during this transformative period that I recognized the profound impact of strategic digital marketing, converting over 25% of online lookers into bookers through different marketing promotional activities. This success ignited my passion for navigating complex regulatory environments and facilitating business growth, ultimately guiding me to a new chapter in my career—law.

Transitioning from hospitality to the legal profession was not just a career shift; it was a response to an emerging need within the industry for someone who comes from this industry, understands its intricacies and nuances and provide solutions commercially and legally. This led me as a legal practitioner to adapt to the evolving landscape shaped by technology, as I founded Darwish Legal Consultants in UAE, my vision expanded beyond traditional legal practice. I realized that in an era defined by rapid technological advancements, the legal profession stands at a pivotal crossroads. The transition from digital tools to artificial intelligence (AI) is not merely a choice; it is an imperative for lawyers aspiring to thrive in an ever-evolving landscape.

Digital solutions have served as a vital first step, enabling legal practitioners to streamline operations, enhance client communication, and improve research capabilities. However, as client expectations grow and the demand for efficiency escalates, the legal profession must embrace a more profound transformation. The integration of AI offers the potential to automate routine tasks, such as document review and contract analysis, significantly reducing the time spent on administrative duties. This newfound efficiency allows lawyers to redirect their focus toward strategic, high-value activities that require their expertise, ultimately leading to improved service and satisfaction for clients.

Moreover, the vast amounts of data generated in legal proceedings create an opportunity for AI to analyze patterns and trends that would be nearly impossible for humans to discern. By leveraging predictive analytics, lawyers can make informed decisions, anticipate client needs, and develop strategies aligned with market dynamics. This data-driven insight becomes increasingly critical as clients demand personalized and responsive services. Today's clients expect not only expertise but also engagement, and AI-powered chatbots and virtual assistants can significantly enhance interactions by providing instant responses to inquiries, scheduling appointments, and delivering timely updates.

The cost-effectiveness of AI cannot be overlooked either. In an era of fierce competition, clients are more discerning than ever, seeking affordable legal solutions without sacrificing quality. By incorporating AI, firms can reduce overhead costs associated with manual processes and pass those savings on to clients, thus gaining a competitive edge. Furthermore, AI has the power to democratize legal services, making them more accessible to individuals and small businesses that may not have the resources to engage traditional legal support. By streamlining processes and lowering costs, we can bridge the justice gap and ensure legal assistance is available to a broader audience.

As I reflect on my journey, I am committed to exploring how AI can revolutionize the legal landscape. At Darwish Legal Consultants, I have integrated cutting-edge digital solutions and AI technologies to enhance our legal services, streamline processes, and provide data-driven insights that allow us to stay ahead in an increasingly competitive environment.

In this book, "From Digital to AI Intelligence: The Future of Lawyers," I will share insights from my journey and the lessons learned along the way. Together, we will delve into the transformative power of AI in the legal profession, highlighting its potential to reshape how lawyers operate, engage with clients, and deliver value. By embracing these innovations, we can not only enhance our practices but also redefine our roles in the digital age. Join me as we embark on this exciting journey into the future of law, where digital solutions and AI intelligence converge to create unprecedented opportunities for legal professionals. Together, we can navigate the complexities of this new landscape and emerge as champions of innovation in the legal field.

CHAPTER 1: THE IMPACT OF DIGITAL TRANSFORMATION ON LEGAL PRACTICES

1. The Changing Landscape of Law

In the beginning was the word, or the letter, or the image, and those who had the gift to offer them to others were much sought after by all. Today, the end is still in sight. It is not as pertinent as the perception of the impact of digital transformation on the practice of law. There is no longer a single word, letter, or image that summarises our thoughts, feelings, and intentions. Our creations are now distributed, usually instantly and often globally. Do those who produce products that result from thought and creativity still hold the power to restiveness in a world in which the true seats of both money and power? We practice a version of the law that would be recognizable to the educated of a hundred years ago. The matters that fall into our purview today had been anticipated and canvassed decades ago by people half a world away, but the conditions necessary for legal practice had not yet materialized.

1.1. The role of technology in modern legal practices

The use of technology in legal practices has been on the increase, thanks to blockchain, AI, the internet, cloud services, and big data analysis technology. An increasing number of lawyers are now attempting to automate business contacts and legal documents. Technology is also used in billable tasks like e-discovery and legal research. Legal practices are also using chatbots to offer users quick access to rudimentary legal information. By doing so, law practices can decrease legal costs by increasing the speed, efficiency, and accuracy of their legal service rendering. In this context, it is important to consider whether there is a need to change the traditional concepts of the practice of law, the rules of professional conduct, and the attorney-client privilege to allow artificial intelligence to replace human decision-making processes.

The American Bar Association issued a report that identified the future changes in technology and their likely impact on legal practices. These included the increasing use of blockchain. Ubiquitous internet access and the use of smartphones and mobile solutions have encouraged access to online legal services across borders, and this trend is expected to grow. Although online legal service has been around for some time, it has not taken the place of an attorney. However, non-lawyers have formed companies and are offering customers the creation of legal documents or providing legal information. The development of AI and data mining is leading to machines providing more and more legal services similar to those provided by attorneys. As a result, there must be a rethinking of the current regulatory structure for legal practices in order to provide individuals, lawyers, and the court system the assurance that non-human legal services have the same level of protection as human legal services. In the UK, the Law Society has undertaken an appraisal of legal services rendered through AI. It has confirmed that the time is now right for the use of AI in the legal field and that its use needs to be embraced.

1.2. key technologies transforming the legal sector

The ongoing digital transformation is creating novel revenue channels, opening alternative ways of providing legal services, and revolutionizing corporate and financial transactions. To keep up with these modifications, legal professionals need to acquire high abilities to manage the reform at all levels. The main needs are (1) improving digital standards and maturity of business procedures, (2) having a positive approach and beginning a cooperation culture with legal technology businesses, and (3) a tailored reorganization of firm layouts and competencies embracing the legal technology guidelines made by global centers.

The title of a report summarizes some stages of the ongoing digital transformation of the legal sector. In particular, the preface and some chapters represent the impact of digital technologies on private equity, mentioning new inputs created by social capital in the legal sector, the increasing customer awareness driven by better use of dashboards and key performance indicators, and the evolution of lawyers' personal relationships influenced by the continuing digital transformation. These goals can be achieved in every international location where professional firms motivate and include the best available knowledge to optimize such legal industry production factors. In this view, as in other areas, we affirm that:

In the legal sector, technological innovation accelerates thought performance by about six times and amplifies the magnitude of thinking tasks performed by practitioners. This conclusion powerfully impacts human behavioural considerations with the economic and legislative repercussions of the traditional legal profession. That is the paradigm shift that embarks on the digital transformation of the legal industry. The identification of the key digital technologies transforming the legal sector is important to design the managerial strategies to follow.

2. Benefits and Challenges of Digital Transformation

Digital tools and technologies have the potential to deliver a myriad of benefits to legal practices. Time and cost efficiencies, enhanced access to legal services, improved client satisfaction, and process automation are among the top-mentioned advantages. Process efficiencies that will lead to improved client services, as well as enhanced access to knowledge to develop winning strategies, are key benefits of using technology in legal practices. Around 60 percent of respondents considered that one of the main benefits of using technology in the practice of law was to reduce the cost of operation. Early deployment of technology can also potentially reduce operational overheads and deliver services to clients faster, thus offering a direct alternative to legal service delivery in terms of legal costs and outcomes.

In responding to how technology can benefit legal practices, a challenging threat to the status quo ways of developing and delivering legal services is posed. Technology can dramatically reduce costs and time delays between presenting different cases in legal systems. Digital tools are seen as providing the means to transform traditional methods of dispute resolution and the way legal services are delivered. An ability to prove the concept of developing a national dispute resolution system and ways to enhance productivity is cited as key benefits of embracing technology and digital tools. Resistance to the use of digital tools in resolving legal cases is identified as a challenge. Ethical standards and regulating the use of digital tools in delivering legal services are proposed as important to ensure that procedural fairness is not compromised.

Regulatory intervention is suggested as a way of promoting the beta trial use of software in legal matters by vulnerable people. Existing regulatory regimes may produce the necessary ethical and professional safeguards to ensure that lawyers use technology in legal service delivery safely. Discussions on ethical standards occur in many ethical codes for legal practitioners who have started to consider the implications of technologies like cognitive computing. Managing change involving the use of digital tools in service delivery is an issue within legal firms, as resistance to change is noted as a challenge to educating clients and lawyers on the virtues of transformative technologies. Assistive legal technologies are often not adopted due to perceptions of job losses among legal professionals.

Yet, there is resistance based on the idea that benchmarks for good lawyering lie with crafting a persuasive argument and a deep understanding of the law and its surrounding ecosystem. This perspective trivializes the use of digital tools that can perform the functions of fact-finding, law and fact application, and assist clients in the conduct of litigation. Further, to the extent that technologies may be considered inferior in outcomes to human endeavors and litigation strategies, this may be outweighed by the transformative nature of such tools in creating new types of legal service delivery. Embraced digital tools can move legal practice from a content-based approach to an outcome and user-based context. Thus, perceived usefulness and preferences for human intervention-based services in the longer term will start to dominate, informing attitudes towards technology's role in future legal service delivery.

3. Consequences Of Ignoring Digital Marketing

Non-responders ignore these new promotional channels at their peril. More and more potential customers are using the internet to find products and services and to research before making a purchase. Without an online presence, these customers won't even find out that businesses exist. For most websites, over 80% of visitors to their sites come to them via the search engines and online directories. With search engines becoming the first place people look for information, SEO and good exposure in the search engines are critical in driving traffic to a site. This form of marketing can generate huge numbers of visitors to a website and can cause sales to soar. A strong social media presence is also crucial to driving traffic. Without being present on social media websites, businesses are missing out on a large portion of the population that is using these sites.

Ultimately, however, if consumers don't know about businesses and the products or services that are provided, they are not going to follow through with a purchase. The traditional marketing approach is no longer as effective, and many customers are turning their attention away from traditional advertising and are beginning to engage with social media and internet advertising campaigns. It is important to keep ahead of the competition, and failure to do so can lead to lost opportunities as well as lost market share. Most businesses either believe or would be surprised to find out that there is a clear correlation with the growth in online engagement and decision making. A number of case studies offer evidence that by shying away from online marketing and embracing traditional approaches, businesses will struggle to gain the same results their competitors are achieving. The days of booster clubs and subscription adverts are slowly fading away. Advertisers may lose significant amounts annually to ineffective campaigns due to poor targeting and segmentation as they fail to adapt to online marketing. Throughout the economy, and without an online customer base, financial loss is almost an eventuality. It is worth reiterating here that one of the main forms of propaganda for digital marketing is the non-negotiable outreach to adapting a business model that incorporates what the consumer really wants.

Consumers don't know about businesses and the products or services offered, they are unlikely to make a purchase. This highlights the growing importance of effective outreach in today's competitive landscape. The traditional marketing approach, heavily reliant on physical advertisements or word of mouth, is no longer as effective. A prime example of this is **Blockbuster**, which failed to embrace the rise of digital marketing and online streaming, instead sticking to outdated strategies. Meanwhile, companies like **Netflix** leveraged online engagement, using targeted social media campaigns and personalized recommendations to capture consumer attention. Blockbuster's inability to adapt quickly resulted in significant losses and ultimately its collapse.

Similarly, many customers are now turning their attention away from traditional advertising and are engaging with social media and internet campaigns, as seen with **Airbnb**. The company understood that its audience was increasingly online and shifted its marketing to focus on platforms like Instagram, where it shared user-generated content and targeted advertisements. This approach allowed Airbnb to achieve rapid growth and dominate the market, while competitors relying solely on traditional advertising fell behind.

Failure to adapt to these digital trends can lead to missed opportunities and lost market share. This is evident in the case of **Toys "R" Us**, which, despite its long-standing brand, continued to focus on physical stores and traditional marketing. Their resistance to embracing e-commerce and digital advertising allowed competitors like **Amazon** to swoop in with targeted online campaigns and more convenient shopping experiences, leading to Toys "R" Us' bankruptcy.

The correlation between growth in online engagement and decision-making is clear. Studies show that businesses leveraging online platforms, social media, and data-driven marketing see greater results in sales and customer retention than those relying on outdated methods. Advertisers who fail to adapt to online marketing, like Toys "R" Us, often face financial loss due to ineffective targeting and segmentation. The days of relying solely on traditional booster clubs and subscription ads are fading fast, and those that don't make the shift are left with dwindling revenues.

Without an online customer base and digital marketing strategy, financial loss becomes inevitable. Businesses that resist this change often see a decline in consumer interest, as modern customers expect a personalized and accessible online presence. Therefore, adapting a business model to include what consumers really want—an online experience—is no longer negotiable. The economic landscape shows time and again that digital marketing is the key to staying competitive and relevant in today's market.

4. Consequences of Ignoring AI Solutions

Failing to make use of AI in a company's workflow leaves it at a loss in every aspect of its business operations. Any market is a battleground for all the companies working within it. The victors are those who can perform their activities most effectively and innovate faster than their rivals. AI-powered software solutions can significantly boost employee performance by automating monotonous task performance. This takes the hassle of such activities off their employees' hands and enables them to concentrate on the more imaginative, inventive, and human-centric projects that cannot be left to AI. AI-augmented analytics help businesses make smarter, more data-driven decisions. Analytics based on AI turn insights into viable activity ideas, speed up the development of scenarios during organizational adjustments, and forecast consumer response during market changes.

Simply put, lack of AI leads to ineffective operational optimization and restricted scalability. AI software in business has a big impact on investments that any organization makes. Companies can save on resource costs and dependence by integrating AI-based position tracking and route optimization applications. The lack of any such intelligent operations management platform would cause inefficiencies and increased operational costs. Businesses use AI to enhance client relationships, data protection, and conversion optimization procedures. Ignoring the potential impact of AI technologies might be the start of customer experience issues. To stay competitive, businesses must work to personalize their relationships with their potential prospects and customers. AI capabilities might be vital in assisting businesses in achieving better conversion and revenue generation. The importance of AI for business is well demonstrated by firms' inability to answer customer questions in a timely and personalized manner. A significant percentage of businesses are reluctant to utilize AI in their organizations, costing them their market relevance significantly. One of the companies that has started developing an automated chatbot system for handling customer queries in order to catch up and fulfill customers' demands, the first chatbot, **ELIZA**, was developed by **Joseph Weizenbaum** at MIT in 1966. ELIZA mimicked a psychotherapist by using simple scripts to engage in conversation with users. While it wasn't used commercially, ELIZA demonstrated the potential of automated conversational systems, laying the groundwork for future chatbot developments.

In a commercial context, **SmarterChild**, developed in the early 2000s by ActiveBuddy, was one of the first chatbots to be widely recognized. It was deployed on platforms like AOL Instant Messenger and MSN Messenger, where it provided interactive responses for entertainment and basic information retrieval. While SmarterChild was a precursor to modern AI-powered assistants, it demonstrated how automated interactions could engage users and drive more frequent platform use, though specific sales or retention impacts were not well-documented at the time.

The rise of AI-driven chatbots, such as **Siri**, **Google Assistant**, and **Alexa**, has had a significant impact on customer service and retention. Companies leveraging these bots have seen improved customer satisfaction and retention rates, as chatbots enable 24/7 service, quick response times, and personalized interactions. Studies show that chatbots can reduce customer service costs by up to 30% and increase user engagement, ultimately boosting customer retention and sales by providing immediate and effective responses to customer queries.

CHAPTER 2: DIGITAL PRESENCE FOR LAWYERS: BUILDING VISIBILITY AND TRUST IN A NOISY WORLD

1. Introduction to Digital Marketing for Advocates

You've worked hard as an advocate, learning everything you can about your cause and strategies for making a difference. Now, how do you make sure people hear what you have to say? You need to meet your audience where they are, and that's online. It's not enough to just be online; you need a strategy for how to do your best work and get what you have to say in front of those who will find it valuable. That's where digital marketing comes in. The key strategies and tools in digital marketing can help you grow your cause, reach and activate new audiences, and grow your organization. In this webinar, you will learn about the process of attracting your community and supporters to your organization's website, your social media channels, and your email list.

If your organization has limited resources, a digital marketing strategy is crucial. Building an online presence is different from traditional advocacy. Digital marketing is a unique blend of marketing and advocacy, and the strategies used in for-profit marketing are just as useful in campaigning and advocacy. Your communications need to be short, easily understood, and resonant with your audience. You will ensure that your hard work will have the most impact when you apply digital marketing tools to reach those who would most value and use what you have to offer them.

1.1 Definition and Importance of Digital Marketing For Advocates

Digital marketing is a broad term that encompasses numerous ways of interacting with customers and clients, including traditional ones like print ads and billboards, and modern ones such as websites and social media. The main point is that digital marketing is any marketing effort using a digital device or the internet. Note that how we use these devices has shifted over the years, and so has the meaning of digital marketing. In the past, it often referred to using the internet for online commerce, for instance, buying books or clothing from an online store. Then social media emerged, and its use grew to the scale that required attention. Brands recognized the potential of an always-on audience and started reallocating marketing dollars from print and TV ads to social media ads. Now state governments are recognizing the presence of the internet and a soon-to-be always-connected population and are designing laws for which no one quite knows the consequences, both positive and negative.

With people huddling to get as much of the internet as quickly as we can in remote areas and cities alike, and with no clear guidelines or rules to protect information and identity that is being served in expensive areas to otherwise voiceless people, we should not hesitate not only to take advantage of the tools being offered to us but to get involved with their offering, to question where they are taking us and to what purpose. In the realm of internet offerings and hammering the marketing nail with a marketing hammer, the meaning and importance of digital marketing pales in comparison to freedom of expression and democratic values. Still, digital marketing is a tool used, including by advocates, and in this sense, we should all become familiar with its use and potential consequences.

2. Understanding the Advocacy Landscape

Whether you are an advocate for an entire issue, a person, or an organization, there are digital components to every modern advocacy approach. It is rare to find a relevant a law or legal consultancy firm without a website, and rarer still to find one that has not dipped its toes into social media. Digital marketing is not meant to replace the core mission of an advocacy organization—building widespread grassroots support for specific issue areas with specific policy goals—but is essential to attaining the reach it takes to garner that support. Successful digital marketing engages others based on what they are interested in, what they are going to do, and what they care about, and how that aligns with advancing the organization's strategic plan.

When advocacy becomes policy, digital marketing can help an organization build culture around the success, show support has changed behaviors, and develop a business model to fund more advocacy. Digital marketing defines a target audience as a person whose characteristics make them especially receptive to having a policy change and having clearly defined values and preferences related to emotional or psychological motivations towards the advocacy ask.

2.1 Types of Advocacy Organizations

Advocacy organizations can be categorized according to the types of advocacy they perform and the goals they accomplish. When examining your specific digital marketing needs and overall approach to advocacy, consider what type of advocacy organization you are working for and what your mission is. In digital marketing, understanding how your advocacy organization is categorized can help clarify what type of goals you are trying to accomplish and what challenges you may encounter. In some situations, advocacy organizations may participate in more than one type of advocacy, and therefore may have a more complex digital marketing plan. It's worth noting that no organization strictly falls into one category. Most advocacy agencies would generally engage in client relationship and physical business development rather than reaching clients through other digital channels.

2.2 Target Audiences in Advocacy

It is important to identify and understand your target audience in advocacy since it creates the opportunity to formulate effective marketing strategies. The target audience could range from policymakers, community leaders, the private sector, civil society organizations, to the general public. When it comes to advocacy, the target audiences are usually divided into two parts: those whom you are trying to influence (primary) and those who can help amplify your message to the targeted primary audience (secondary). The most important part of this equation is the primary audience, who has the decision-making power on a specific issue, as this represents the target of the advocacy campaign.

Once the target audience has been identified, information about this audience—what they feel, how they think, and the constraints they operate in—will be the guiding light in the communication campaign that an advocacy strategy requires. Understanding who the stakeholders are in an issue is also crucial—people who can stop the advocacy campaign in its tracks because they have the power to prevent progress or will otherwise be a barrier to the change required.

3. Key Strategies for Building an Online Presence

As you prepare to build an online presence, it is important to have an understanding of the various platforms and tools available to organizations today. Selecting the right ones for your organization will depend on a number of factors. For one, understanding what your strategic objectives are will determine which platforms will be the most beneficial to meet those goals. Other considerations include having a clear understanding of your supporters and which online platforms they are using the most. In the modern technological era, people and the forums in which they express themselves – and absorb information – are constantly in flux. The digital tools and strategies available to the modern advocacy organization to spread its word are varied to say the least. What's more, these vehicles keep changing at an ever-quickening pace. And their mutations add layers of complexity to what is already a tough nut to crack when trying to measure their respective impacts.

3.1 Developing a Strong Brand Identity

Digital Marketing Essentials for Advocates: Key Strategies for Building an Online Presence Whether you run a non-profit organization or find yourself leading the communications or marketing department of an international NGO, your challenge is the same – how do you make sure that your organization stands out and is noticed among the thousands of others that work within similar sectors or on similar causes? Your challenge is to amplify your work and bring ideas to the attention of those who matter. As such, we thought that we would compile our knowledge and share it with others to help make your life easier. So what does your brand stand for? Well, that's pretty much what your brand is. It's the most recognizable way of differentiating yourself from another. It is your identity and, while a brand doesn't convey all your values and beliefs, it does give a sneak peek into who you are and what separates you from the rest. Your brand is comprised of a brand mark (name, logo, symbols, and other distinctive imagery), along with a set of promises that represent key messages that, at their best, will come to symbolize what you stand for. The key to creating a strong brand identity is knowing who you are and what you represent. Your story needs to be authentic, and from it, you should build a brand that reflects who you are, what you do, and what you believe. Imagine that your brand is a person. This person should be well-dressed, well-groomed, have character, and have such distinctive attributes that make him or her easily identifiable. They should greet people when they meet them, remember details about them, and treat them with the respect they deserve.

A good example of a person with a strong personal brand and a recognizable logo is Michael Jordan. His brand, represented by the iconic Jumpman logo, reflects who he is: a legendary basketball player known for excellence, discipline, and winning. The Jumpman silhouette, derived from Jordan's signature dunk, has become synonymous with his athletic prowess and transcends sports, extending into lifestyle and fashion through collaborations with Nike's Air Jordan line.

Jordan's personal brand is not just about performance; it embodies leadership and aspiration, attracting fans and consumers worldwide.

The Jumpman logo began as part of a transactional marketing strategy focused on promoting Michael Jordan's partnership with Nike through the Air Jordan sneaker line, first launched in 1984. Nike initially aimed to leverage Jordan's rising popularity to sell shoes to basketball fans. However, this strategy evolved into relationship marketing by understanding its audience deeply and appealing to multiple generations. As Jordan's career progressed, the brand didn't just market shoes; it embodied his values of excellence, perseverance, and cultural influence.

The Jumpman logo became legendary not only because of Jordan's unmatched athletic achievements but also through the brand's ability to adapt its messaging over the years. Nike and the Jordan brand cultivated a lifestyle identity that extended beyond sports, associating the logo with fashion, music, and street culture. Unlike many other sports icons that faded, the Jumpman stayed relevant by aligning with changing trends and embracing collaborations with newer generations, such as partnerships with artists and athletes.

This ability to blend timeless symbolism with modern relevance has ensured that the logo never lost its cultural significance. It became not just a mark of quality but a status symbol, embraced across generations—from those who witnessed Jordan's prime to younger audiences who recognize the brand's legacy through storytelling and contemporary endorsements.

3.2 Creating Compelling Content

Michael Jordan and the Jordan Brand provide a perfect example of how creating engaging content can amplify a brand's digital presence. Over time, Jordan's personal story and brand have informed, engaged, and inspired a global audience through strategic storytelling on digital platforms.

One of the brand's key strategies was to ask questions and engage its audience directly. Through interactive campaigns—like asking fans to share their personal "Jordan moments" or opinions on new sneaker releases—the brand created a two-way dynamic. This interaction fostered a sense of community and loyalty, making consumers feel personally connected to the brand.

The use of data has also been central to Jordan's digital presence. Infographics about the performance of Air Jordans or visual representations of Jordan's career stats have added credibility and kept the audience engaged. These visual tools not only highlight the brand's roots in athletic excellence but also position it as a knowledgeable leader in both sportswear and lifestyle branding.

Additionally, testimonials from other athletes, celebrities, and even everyday consumers have reinforced the Jordan Brand's impact. Videos and social media posts featuring testimonials from new brand ambassadors like Zion Williamson, as well as collaborations with high-profile figures such as Travis Scott and Virgil Abloh, demonstrate the brand's adaptability and relevance in contemporary culture. For instance, the Air Jordan 1 x Travis Scott collaboration not only blended streetwear and basketball culture but also generated massive buzz, selling out almost instantly and solidifying the brand's status as a cultural phenomenon. These testimonials don't just highlight product performance—they communicate why wearing Jordans is a symbol of belonging to a larger cultural movement.

Therefore, one of the most important steps in going digital is creating compelling content that will inform, engage, and inspire your audience. While it can take time to figure out exactly what type of content works best for your specific goals and audience, here are some useful formulas for creating highly engaging social media content.

- **Ask Questions** Simply asking questions is an incredibly powerful way to get your audience engaged. By asking a question, you are not only asking people to consider their own thoughts, but also allowing them to share those thoughts with you. This creates a two-way dynamic that can help your content have a lasting impact.

• **Use Data Infographics and data visualizations** are some of the most shareable content formats for a good reason. Not only can they package dense information in an easy-to-understand format, but they can also help position your organization as a reputable source of information.

• **Share Testimonials** Getting people involved in your work can be the most powerful way to share your message. By sharing why others support your cause, you can show new audiences why they should too.

3.3 Leveraging Social Media Platforms

Social media platforms are an effective tool for quickly reaching a vast audience and are easy to use and manage. These well-known platforms for individuals and corporates are especially great for regular, bite-sized updates, but the key to making these sites work for you is regular, high-quality updates and time devoted to building your audience. Consistency is key to social media and to increasing your audience. As accounts become more active, user engagement and growth increase over time. Facebook and Twitter are great for quick updates, links to longer pieces, and discussion. Pinterest is very visual and is used primarily to share web images. YouTube and Vimeo are great for video sharing. LinkedIn has a more professional tone and is good for updates related to work, a resume, and business networking. Tumblr is a content creation platform that is a rich source for high-quality images, although the social component is somewhat limited. Google+ is an emerging platform with impressive potential. Blog posts and content can be displayed for a share-happy audience. Sharing is key. Always link back to your original content, wherever it is located on your website, blog, or video channel. The more links back to your site, the higher your site will appear in search engine results.

The strategic use of social media by advocacy firms not only enhances their visibility but also empowers their employees and lawyers to generate business opportunities. For example, Fisher Phillips has encouraged its attorneys to participate actively on platforms like LinkedIn, allowing them to showcase their expertise and engage with a broader audience. This not only positions the individual lawyers as thought leaders but also drives potential clients to the firm. By amplifying their attorneys' voices through social media, the firm capitalizes on the influence that personal branding can have on client perception.

Similarly, Baker McKenzie has developed a culture of content sharing, where its lawyers regularly contribute articles, insights, and commentary on current legal issues. This strategy not only promotes the firm but also helps the lawyers establish their credibility in specific practice areas. As these attorneys become recognized figures in their respective fields, the firm benefits from the trust and authority that these individuals build, leading to new business opportunities.

Skadden, Arps, Slate, Meagher & Flom LLP takes this a step further by using social media to highlight individual attorneys' achievements and their contributions to high-profile cases. This approach creates a narrative around the firm's expertise and showcases its lawyers as capable leaders in their areas of practice. As their lawyers gain visibility and respect through consistent social media engagement, it opens doors to client relationships and referrals that might not have materialized otherwise.

These firms demonstrate that the "noise" created through marketing and social media engagement can significantly influence public perception and business development. When attorneys share valuable insights, engage with industry discussions, and present themselves as knowledgeable professionals, they not only enhance their personal brands but also contribute to the firm's reputation. This dual impact underscores the importance of a cohesive social media strategy that encourages participation from all levels within the firm.

CHAPTER 3: DIGITAL MARKETING ESSENTIALS FOR ADVOCATES

Static websites are no longer an option, if you want your website to work in your favor. You need a site that is always evolving, always engaging, always transforming. Since you might not have a huge budget for this website, there are some restrictions we will work within, the main one being that you need to be able to update the website yourself. While more social change-oriented groups should not likely attempt building the website themselves, even nonprofits can achieve a more polished look without a huge outlay through website templates, theme design, and a little help from a contractor or two. Sometimes, a mix of free tools and some paid help can make everything come together rather nicely. These are really good and really bad times for the organizations that have a mix of rich media text and deep archives of information such as reports, films, and podcasts.

The good news is that there are more free internet tools than I can count that make it simple for advocates like you to add audio, video, and photo galleries to your website. This, added to low-cost web hosting services, means showcasing your assets does not have to eat up your web budget. The bad news is, of course, you still need someone to build your website with these features and manage your content. One of the solutions for organizations feeling constrained by proprietary back-end software and concomitant time involvement in reformatting your pre-digital archives might be WordPress.

Absolutely, small advocacy firms can leverage these digital strategies to compete effectively with larger firms, and the evolving nature of websites plays a crucial role in this. Static websites simply won't cut it anymore; they need to be dynamic and constantly engaging to attract and retain visitors. Not to compete with the large advocacy organizations but to act similar or to have a seat among them.

While budget constraints might limit options, it's entirely feasible for smaller firms to maintain an updated, professional-looking website. Utilizing website templates and platforms like WordPress can provide a polished appearance without breaking the bank. Many advocacy organizations are successfully combining free tools with some paid assistance to create engaging sites that showcase their initiatives effectively.

For example, adding rich media content like videos, podcasts, and photo galleries can significantly enhance user engagement. These elements not only draw attention but also help to tell a compelling story about the organization's mission and impact. With numerous low-cost hosting services available, advocacy groups can present their resources without draining their budget. If you do not how to use these tools yourlsef, you may check the freelance websites that serves your geographical location and you may find someone who can help you build a professional looking website according to your needs and the practicing law you or your advocacy firm do, and they can show you the how to add content to the website through the backend interface. This will help you start having a professional optimum looking that can make you feel that you paved the way towards your future legal presence.

Moreover, the ability for staff and lawyers to contribute to the website's content can amplify the firm's presence. By sharing insights, experiences, and testimonials, they transform into brand advocates themselves, which is especially potent for smaller firms looking to make their mark

1. Design and User Experience Principles

The theme of visual design and user interface may seem quite different, but they are interconnected. When you are designing a website, it is vital to keep in mind who it is for and why the user makes certain decisions. Perhaps it is a website to be utilized by scientists, with a target group in the 50-60 year age range, or perhaps your site is designed for active women who want to use a website to plan an exciting outdoor adventure. Whatever your target group, a visual look should be targeted for them to go to. If you can, get some of the members you identified and have a usage session. Check out the layout of the original paper sketches as well as the more accurate mock-ups. Lay out the paper sketches onto newsprints or cardboards and ask the users to try to use the site, giving them scenario-based tasks you are developing. The tasks demonstrate each page's features and help the user execute different expectations. These sessions are invaluable, as you get input from those who will finally use the product.

2. Search Engine Optimization (SEO) Basics

One of the most powerful things you can do to help your cause rise in search engine results is to regularly produce quality content. The best way to do this is to host a blog on your website. A blog is a living, breathing part of your website; a place where you can post written articles, video content, polls, and feature guest bloggers. The content you provide should be useful and relevant to your audience, related to your cause, regularly updated, and well written. The more rich, keyword-focused content you produce, the better your overall website will perform in searches.

In order to keep people coming back to your site and to encourage sharing of your content, you'll want to produce quality shareable content or article each week. The best way to get your blog noticed and picked up by search engines' algorithms is to create SEO-focused content. SEO is a powerful way of driving traffic to your website. SEO is the practice of improving and promoting a website in order to increase the number of visitors the site receives from search engines. There is a fine art to SEO, but when mastered it can lead to a lifetime of advocacy results. In short, good SEO practices should include solid keyword placement, keyword focus, keyword-optimized titles, meta tags, and descriptions, and utilize website navigation that is logically set up.

3. Email Marketing and Advocacy

Email marketing and advocacy often go hand in hand. However, the key to successful email marketing is less about sending out emails than it is about being strategic when you do send out your emails. In this section, we're going to break down that strategy and explore effective forms of email marketing for advocacy.

Email Segmentation put simply; your email list includes all of your email subscribers. This is table stakes when it comes to A/B testing and running splits for the sake of that experiment. You can have as many segments as you see fit, but several to consider include activists from a specific region, greater donors, and general email addresses. However, if you're a group that focuses on multiple issues, then your list might include subgroups of voters who only engage on certain issues. Some organizations use email to provide regular updates on the continued impact of the work they do, whereas others are amazing at using photography to think visually and sometimes have actions built around special causes important to their members.

3.1 Building an Email List

Without question, one of the most important aspects of digital influence, particularly for advocates, is the ability to directly reach your community members. With many social media platforms changing their algorithms regularly, your community members may not always see your posts unless you spend advertising dollars. Mailing lists are by far the most effective way to directly reach a large group of contacts quickly and to convey important, specific messages to your community members. It's easy to think that in the age of 140-character tweets, lengthy email communications are passé, but as a matter of fact, many effective digital advocacy campaigns have been carried out primarily through email communications. Especially when compared to the constantly changing algorithms of social media platforms, email campaigns and communications are relatively straightforward to plan and execute. On social media, your followers are likely to miss your communications, supplied only sporadically and with algorithms that limit the reach of your communications from time to time. Depending solely on your social media platforms to communicate your message to your community members also means missing the potential of many other reliable tools in relation to the effectiveness of your outreach. This growth in efficiency can happen in a number of ways, such as in person at other advocacy events or online. Your website can be a primary source or a catch-all for people who want to express support and potentially join your mailing list.

3.2 *Crafting Effective Email Campaigns*

Email is an important tool for advocates in building community, delivering messages, and mobilizing support. It is also a method that reaches audiences while not risking significant privacy issues. As specific rules apply to email campaigns, organizations should keep in communication and be professional.

Valid email lists are paramount. Gather this information from business cards, ask your LinkedIn followers to provide you with their email to list them in your email campaigns, and other reputable sources. Be upfront with new contacts. Let them know that you are adding them and how to unsubscribe if they wish, this can be done from various third-parties software such as Mail Chimp and Zoho Campaigns which I use in my advocacy firm. After gathering addresses, regularly take steps to confirm that contacts are interested in hearing from you. Failing to do so can leave your messages marked as unwanted spam. Organizations should also include current colleagues or friends in a test run, checking how their messages present when received and ensuring that the messages remain well-formatted throughout.

Further, a MIME-compliant email refers to an email that follows the Multipurpose Internet Mail Extensions (MIME) standard. MIME is a protocol that enables emails to include more than just plain text—such as attachments, images, videos, HTML content, PDF's and special character sets—in a way that is correctly encoded and transmitted over the internet are necessary to reach all inboxes, and they should warn about attaching irrelevant files that may result in the messages being marked as spam. Use text and header formatting to avoid a report as phishing. Additionally, view permissions or usage policies require a check. Are you still allowed to use images or text contained in an email that was sent or received by a specific contact? Rejection rules may prevent messages from reaching a secure destination, so it is important to phrase outreach with caution. All marketing activities must make accommodations that respect legal requirements. Save time and use the above mentioned third-party applications and make it happen.

4. Data Analytics and Reporting

"Data is the new oil," and that is true, especially now with every aspect of campaigning being a scientific approach. Brands use data and analyze reports to the last detail. It is high time our sector partnered with data to make meaningful decisions. Data are important indicators of our campaign success. Quantitative data are the basis of every campaign's primary report. We need to alter indicators that are not simply supported by our quantitative data; such are increased media mentions or an impression share on media being two examples. Although the degree may also vary, the reports in global communications resemble more of the ones the others are deemed as from methodology, print forming to tracking. These reports have to be followed and released by specific timings, usually by the campaign end or by the campaign to ensure the information is correct against our aim; it must be operated as a live control.

4.1 Key Metrics to Track

How do you know if your efforts are paying off? There are a few key success indicators that you can review to consider if you are on the right path. Not all of these are directly related to donations. Fundraising through online community building is a long-term project, and it doesn't always align with immediate financial gain. That's why it's important to track the development of relationships with your online community and the sharing of your content, as both work towards longer-term targets. Some immediate key indicators that you can keep an eye on are usually the obvious ones: How many followers do you have (and how many of them are interacting with your content)? How many people like, share, retweet, or comment on your content? How much website traffic comes from social media? Which traffic source from social media converts the best? While these are nowhere near a full picture of social media success, tracking these indicators will give you some idea of whether or not your efforts are gaining traction and if you're responsive to what your audience wants.

4.2 Tools for Data Analysis

Google Analytics can help lawyers understand how their website is performing, how visitors are finding and engaging with their content, and how they can optimize their site for conversions. For example, lawyers can use Google Analytics to track the number of leads generated from their website, the sources of traffic, the bounce rate, the time spent on the site, the pages visited, and the actions taken. They can also use Google Analytics to set up goals, track events, and measure the return on investment of their online marketing campaigns.

SEMRush can help lawyers improve their search engine optimization (SEO) and online visibility, by providing insights into the keywords, competitors, and trends that drive traffic to their website and their niche. For example, lawyers can use SEMRush to conduct keyword research, analyze their competitors' strategies, monitor their rankings, identify gaps and opportunities, and optimize their content and technical SEO. 5 They can also use SEMRush to audit their website, track their backlinks, and manage their online reputation.

Majestic can help lawyers analyze their backlink profile and identify the quality and relevance of the websites that link to their site. Backlinks are important for SEO, as they signal the authority and trustworthiness of a website to search engines and users. For example, lawyers can use Majestic to discover new link opportunities, monitor their link health, compare their backlink profile with their competitors, and remove or disavow harmful or spammy links that can hurt their rankings.

SimilarWeb can help lawyers benchmark their website performance and compare it with their competitors and industry standards. It can also help lawyers discover new sources of traffic, identify emerging trends and opportunities, and understand their audience behavior and preferences. For example, lawyers can use SimilarWeb to see how their website ranks in their category and country, how their traffic is distributed across different channels and devices, what keywords and topics are driving traffic to their site, and what other websites their visitors are interested in.

Alexa can help lawyers measure their website popularity and influence, as well as gain insights into their target market and competitors. It can also help lawyers optimize their website for user experience and SEO, by providing suggestions and best practices. For example, lawyers can use Alexa to see how their website ranks globally and locally, how their traffic and engagement metrics compare with their competitors, what keywords and topics are relevant for their niche, and how they can improve their site speed, usability, and security.

SE Ranking can help lawyers monitor and improve their SEO performance, by providing a comprehensive and user-friendly platform that covers all aspects of SEO. It can also help lawyers manage their online marketing campaigns, by providing tools for social media, email marketing, and PPC advertising. For example, lawyers can use SE Ranking to track their keyword rankings, analyze their backlinks, audit their website, optimize their on-page SEO, research their competitors, and generate reports and analytics.

DataForSEO Labs can help lawyers explore and experiment with different aspects of SEO, by providing access to various data sets and APIs that can be used for research and testing purposes. It can also help lawyers learn and stay updated with the latest SEO trends and developments, by providing insights and analysis. 16 For example, lawyers can use DataForSEO Labs to see how their website ranks for different keywords, how their competitors are performing, what factors affect their SEO, and what opportunities and challenges they face.

In conclusion, these tools offer a wide range of benefits for lawyers looking to enhance their online presence, improve their SEO performance, and gain valuable insights into their website and audience. By leveraging these tools, lawyers can stay competitive in the digital landscape, attract more clients, and ultimately grow their practice.

CHAPTER 4: LEGAL AND ETHICAL CONSIDERATIONS IN DIGITAL MARKETING FOR LAWYERS

Legal and ethical issues related to digital marketing abound. The digital marketing environment is an evolving area of commerce that, in many respects, is ahead of the law in establishing clear rules. This is in part because the technology and the media themselves are rapidly evolving, but it is also due to the fact that many of the industries and firms operating in the digital arena are relatively new and are still "feeling" their way through the legal and ethical Exploring Future Trends in Legal Technology: What to Expect for the Legal Profession in the Age of AI. Despite the difficulty of creating hard and fast rules that apply to all situations and all parties, digital marketers must understand important principles and consider the potential for a wide range of legal and ethical challenges.

Freedom of speech is a huge part of the First Amendment to the U.S. Constitution. The First Amendment applies to all forms of spoken and written expression and also applies to visual and performing arts and broadcast, online, and social media. For-profit companies can speak through commercial advertising that has both a political and commercial message. Nevertheless, restrictions have been imposed through legislation and regulations to protect the public from false, deceptive, or misleading commercial speech among other reasons. Areas like privacy protection, trademark and copyright protection, e-commerce, and control of advertising targeting vulnerable populations face an evolving, but well-established, body of predominantly federal law.

1. Privacy Regulations

Privacy concerns are at the top of most people's online issues, and new regulations to protect consumers' sensitive digital information are appearing rapidly. In the European Union, regulations were adopted to help guarantee that customers retain ownership of their online data. Enforcement began in May 2018. Consumer privacy is protected through the regulation, which applies to all EU members. It requires any enterprise that works with the personal data of EU citizens to comply with rules protecting consumer data privacy, compelling businesses to be more transparent about the data that is collected from consumers. The regulations also let people opt out of having their data sold. Violating these regulations can introduce a substantial penalty for businesses. The act also goes against the collection of data for children under the age of 16 unless the child's guardian consents.

This is not comprehensive, and indeed the nuances of these laws are important to understand. This is not just important for enterprises, but for you as an individual entrepreneur as well. Governments are increasingly taking steps to ensure that consumers keep control over their online data, and you need to keep this in mind as you work with marketing strategies so that you don't inadvertently run afoul of these rules. When in doubt, verify legal issues with a specialist. As a result of these regulations, you will see digital marketers asking for consents from visitors as charge-free materials and downloads are provided. Email and SMS lists will likely be shrinking as regulations become more robust to democratize data. This is the cost of treasure hunting for customer leads and marketing returns.

2. Transparency and Disclosure

Be open and transparent about yourself on your professional site. Clients will generally look for you online, so provide them with the information they are looking for. It can be beneficial to use social media presences that relate to your title, your professional area of practice, or the activities that you engage in outside of your professional life. Consider adding a professional profile image as well that matches your career, keeping it the same looks and feel on any social media platform regardless the usage of such platform – this way, people who are interested in who you are can put a face to your name, and not only this but the Search Engines such as Google and Yahoo will optimize your photo and it will be indexed faster in any search results and on any Search Engine. Professional openness also means fully filling out your profile. Ensure that all information that is shared in the profile is completed, proofread, and consistent. Any attachments you are sharing should be fully working, live, and up to date. Remember, lawyer regulation may have restrictions: however, be mindful of your local rules. There are many ethical and privacy obligations at the individual state level that you will need to be aware of. Common things to be aware of are: rules concerning the solicitation of new clients and social media communications; restrictions concerning attorney advertising and listings; professional obligation attached to your internet conduct. Remember to regularly update your profile once the professional information has been disclosed, and maintain it. Set up alerts to monitor your profile and check in at the site regularly. You should also consider your professional status and who may access your profile, both now and in the future.

3. Emerging Trends in Digital Advocacy

As digital tools continue to evolve, so too do emerging trends in digital advocacy practice. Building awareness of key areas where digital advocacy practice is changing, and where new strategies and opportunities are emerging, can help advocates optimize how they can adapt and effectively engage and influence policy with the increasing use of digital tools. Changes in the digital landscape are a key way that advocacy is changing. Even if the issues advocates face in the physical world stay the same, the opportunities they have to try and solve those problems grow more dynamic every day when it comes to digital advocacy. Many new technologies help us share our stories; we need to find out which tools most compel our audience – the people who have the power to make the decisions we want to see. Our job is to consistently present compelling digital content for the right audience and to use these tools to set the stage for policy change. As the digital world has evolved, there are several emerging trends in digital advocacy practice that can help advocates not just engage their audience but also induce organization or policy change on legislative, regulatory, or funding priorities.

First, think of all of our blogs, social media pages, and other websites. These are where we collect information that shapes our constituents, members, and the public; relatively few of these sites are optimized for presenting information to policymakers. The solution to a social media challenge, one advocate at a time, quickly becomes a problem and an opportunity for many different advocates. Although it is important to understand the desires of social media, it is also important to construct a coherent universal strategy that we consistently use at every digital touchpoint to produce consistent professional results that create awareness and inspire change. As the new digital tools most advocates use become a permanent part of their strategic toolbox, it is also important to note how message control advocates will change.

4. Artificial Intelligence and Machine Learning

Digital marketing, or digital advocacy, has grown rapidly in recent years with the surge of technology platforms creating opportunities for individuals to gather their communities, complete calls to action, participate in public consultations, and share relevant and timely information ranging from news, political messaging, and ordinances to events and public discussions. This supports the need for a strong digital presence and a clear digital persona. Groups with significant digital presences can more easily activate the public and drive their supporters to take action, such as attending political hearings or pressuring their elected officials in a coordinated and informed manner. With the rise of subscription models at major newspapers and a significant decline in local newsrooms, digital presence becomes a first line of defense for appearing in public knowledge or showing responsibility for certain topics. Monitoring and active response to online commentary make it possible to leverage digital platforms in influential ways.

Artificial intelligence can help understand and categorize who is saying what to whom and where, with some organizations working to assess the nature of online commentary. Changes in sentiment, trolling, or a coordinated deceptive network of bots are some of the ways AI is used to categorize online communication. Social media is considered a recommendation on par with traditional public relations and advertising. Indeed, social media strategy has been regarded as a core part of an overall electoral strategy. With the advent of artificial intelligence and machine learning at an unprecedented rate, quantifying the successes of content messaging has become streamlined. This essay aims to advance the capacity of individuals and organizations seeking to effect change through digital advocacy.

5. Virtual Reality and Augmented Reality

Virtual reality and augmented reality are two closely related technologies that explore new frontiers in transporting experiences. Both virtual reality and augmented reality are digital experiences that require the use of technology, such as headsets or apps that provide immersive experiences. With augmented reality, you mix reality with digital; with virtual reality, the experience is wholly digital. AR allows you to drop digital images into the real world. VR requires a head-mounted device that transports the user into an entirely digitally created environment. Both provide opportunities for engaging and interactive storytelling.

For example, lawyers who handle immigration cases or family law cases could implement AR or VR technology into their intake process. By offering potential clients access to their legal expertise through virtual consultations rather than in-office meetings, potential clients can feel more comfortable discussing sensitive and political issues as lawyers can continue to offer skilled legal advice. Furthermore, VR can be used during client meetings to present exhibits in an engaging way, making an impression on clients who may be more impressed by high-tech presentations. These technologies give clients options that traditional practices cannot.

6. Case Studies and Best Practices

As the team conducting the Creating Advocates pilot HELM Training, we borrowed many of the best practices of digital marketing and then tailored and applied them to the task of creating obvious online champions from our diverse, accomplished, and searching alumni association members. Use the opportunities to tell the story online of the projects that are developed as a result of leveraging your location position, including new partnerships and influential connections to help and reuse open spaces.

Applying the best practices of digital marketing in interesting and personal ways makes the creation of obvious champions work for us in a variety of ways. Perhaps you can use some of our experiences to grow your value with your stakeholders online. Ask for and provide social proof – display and tell who is participating in the process and then give your champions the tools they need to participate in a useful and time-effective way. Openly sharing which Advisory Board members are already actively performing the volunteer engagement tasks of idea collecting, tasking, implementing, and evaluating when a new idea comes in, and other champions step forward to help in their area of interest. Sharing accomplished alumni success stories in email and on the web becomes a lot of fun because champions appreciate the chance to bring concrete benefits to the table, and the open sharing then becomes further social proof of the value and reach of the association network.

7. Successful Digital Advocacy Campaigns

Now that we have examined the various digital strategies, let's put them together and see what successful advocacy campaigns on digital platforms look like. Remember that as you create your own digital strategies and campaigns, they should have your goals in mind. You should know and design for who your audience is, what it is you want to tell them, and what you want them to do. Finally, to develop effective digital strategies and campaigns, you must understand the platforms and how they work. Always plan and create content with every platform's strengths and weaknesses in mind. All of your content should be tailored to maximize the strengths and minimize the weaknesses. Be organized, efficient, disciplined, and consistent. Always have a specific purpose and a well-defined call to action when using digital platforms for advocacy work. Be authentic and credible.

One of the best digital advocacy campaigns comes from a non-profit media company funded by readers, and one of the best reporting on climate change. Their Pulitzer Prize-winning campaign outlined the immense importance of early clear-eyed research, which for a time was denied, even while it made billions for pumping carbon into the atmosphere, denying there was any threat from it, and fighting climate awareness at every turn. Using the first and last frames of the ad or a key phrase as a cover slide is a good way to take advantage of platforms that are well suited to slide presentations. A successful and positive campaign is one of the best case studies to watch the movement and impacts. To stop the Dakota Access Pipeline, there was an organized response with foundational support and ultimate support of Indigenous Women of Standing Rock to stop the "Black Snake."

8. Lessons Learned and Recommendations

Take time to build your website, but don't delay your other online marketing tactics while working on your website. Focus on lots of social media and get to know your analytics, as individual analytics from various social media sites are highly informative. Trying to do so many things at once is hard. The power of video is really important, but actually quite difficult and requires some real talent or a phone. You don't have to do everything yourself. You can outsource many parts of your program, but not the strategy.

A perspective on resources needed to manage your program. You need to be able to monitor and assess a wide variety of channels, so this takes some capacity. Stick with your strategy, as your resources and capabilities evolve. It can be difficult to make this type of shift on the fly. You also need a strong advocate and institutional buy-in. Get your board on board and set up a social media policy. Make sure everyone understands the why behind the how. Effective internal communication, so that everyone has the same message and knows what is going on, is also important. Flexibility is essential, as things change. Finally, do some kind of follow-up. What is the reason for the excitement? Interview your stakeholders and work with your digital manager or outsourced provider to answer the "So what?" to use data in order to guide your new plan. Remember, not being on social media is now seen as behind the times.

CHAPTER 5: THE IMPACT OF ARTIFICIAL INTELLIGENCE ON LEGAL WORK

1. Introduction to Artificial Intelligence in the Legal Field

Several factors are fuelling the increased attention now being focused on artificial intelligence (AI) in the legal field. This opening chapter serves as both an introduction to AI and an introductory depiction for the remainder of this book. AI technologies offer new approaches for legal problem solving. They can accomplish, or support the accomplishment of, several tasks that are part of existing legal industry value chains. These new AI-based practices may supplement existing legal practice but, in some cases, they also may substitute for it, transforming the way in which legal professionals work.

AI is a broad concept, and it has various definitions. This book adopts a broad definition, treating AI as a field of computer science in which machines do tasks that would require human intelligence. In the legal field, AI is a field of research and professional development focusing on the creation of a machine capable of doing a task that would require human intelligence if done by a legal professional or, in some instances, a task a legal professional would typically delegate to a paralegal or support professional. AI is comprised of several technical tasks and fields: machine learning, natural language processing and generation, decision support systems and predictive analytics, and robotics or expert systems. Both artificial intelligence and cognitive systems will be able to elicit knowledge necessary for operating in specific knowledge-based domains, such as law.

2. Current Applications of AI in Legal Work

AI has the potential to help legal professionals with a range of work tasks and make law firms more efficient. This chapter gives an overview of some of the current applications of AI within the legal sector. It provides an exploration of the use of AI for document review tasks and how AI is shaping applications that support predictive analytics. This chapter also explores the uptake of AI by industry for machine translation services, integration of chatbots and virtual assistants, as well as dedicated legal research and contract management tools.

The scale of the use of AI in legal work is indicated through a series of case studies and the processes that AI now supports. For example, AI may now support a lawyer by digesting the research output of a junior colleague. AI is transforming the legal profession by streamlining tasks, improving efficiency, and reducing costs. One of the primary areas where AI is making a significant impact is in document review. Tools like *Relativity* and *Everlaw* use AI for e-discovery, sorting through vast volumes of legal documents to identify relevant information in a fraction of the time it would take a human. This allows legal teams to focus on higher-level strategic work, as the time-consuming task of document review is largely automated.

The ability to automate the pastiche or pedantic work is resulting in a change of duties within law firms. Some suggestions exist that this technology should also be capable of challenging the business model of some aspects of corporate law due to its capacity to quickly and accurately provide a range of insights in mergers and acquisition cases. These tools may also be used by independent legal professionals

The impacts of AI in legal work are only just beginning to be conceptualized as the capacities develop, but to remain relevant for contemporary discussions, the potential downside of this technology is considered too. For example, the increased use of AI chatbots in the first instance for client inquiries is like automated attendant facilities. However, because many companies are seeking to insert fictions and deceit, often from a second language position in the first instance, we are speaking to machines and not humans — with all the legal, linguistic, and privacy implications that these carries. This has led many companies to state when asked that they do use this technology, but they assert that it is an independent standard of inquiry if they are using a human, bot, or combined human-bot system. This automated attendant system can be cheaper and faster if the number of spoken language queries can be shifted over the well-maintained script of a chatbot. There is also the danger of reducing the international labor market to the lowest possible common denominator rather than the active recruitment of individuals from conflicting cultural backgrounds who have a high level of fluency in a low demand spoken language.

AI's ability to automate significant portions of legal work is prompting a re-evaluation of traditional law firm business models. Some legal analysts suggest that AI could disrupt the billable hour model, particularly for tasks like document review, legal research, and contract management that can be automated. Clients are increasingly expecting more transparent pricing structures and faster turnaround times, leading firms to adopt fixed-fee models or subscription-based pricing for AI-powered services.

Real-life examples of this shift include firms like Clifford Chance, which has developed its own AI tools to streamline internal processes and provide more competitive pricing to clients. In the long term, this could lead to the restructuring of corporate law services, with firms focusing more on advisory and strategy work, while AI handles much of the administrative burden.

3. The Benefits of AI in Enhancing Efficiency

Artificial intelligence enhances efficiency by automating repetitive work, saving legal professionals time, and decreasing the opportunity costs of monitoring cases in a high-speed commercial legal environment. Document automation systems are being used to train contracts and make the process of entering into contracts more efficient, saving countless hours and significantly reducing deal costs. Similar tools were designed to dissect and gamify contract review. The AI legal research tool allows attorneys to gain efficiencies in research by conducting natural language searches and pulling relevant information from across case law, legislation, secondary resources, and other materials. A firm has reported significant time savings using the tool.

According to a colleague, "When analysis shows certain specific patterns in data or the way humans are interacting with particular systems, first-line responders can be automatically alerted to look more closely at their work. *CaseFlow* provides significantly better legal service than traditional legal services by automating standard document generation, streamlining workflows, improving communication with the use of chatbots, and triaging the legal needs of over 10,000 clients a year." In addition to improving efficiency, analytics uses AI to unearth significant success rates in judges and originality in facts for litigators. AI can also increase data reliability and reduce human errors because algorithms are trained on large sets of data and rationally apply their respective learned data algorithms, leading to more reliable outcomes. It is being used in courtrooms to predict sanctions that follow lawyers. More broadly, continuous learning and adaptation is a feature of AI systems. Automating and learning discrete tasks based on collected data — including text analytics, data mining, and other functionalities — can often result in system upgrades and faster efficiencies. These outputs from AI technology have provided firms with a significant competitive advantage and are increasingly being deemed necessary to remain viable players in the legal market today.

4. AI's Role in Improving Client Service

AI-driven improvements in client service can be integrated into all levels of client interactions, resulting in improved access to justice and providing the ability for larger law firms to provide smoother handoffs between work areas and reduce potential situations of conflict. The development of a sophisticated client AI interface is being used to great effect by a specialist care legal firm as a public resource and is now being further tested for internal use. The implementation has led to a change in the collaborative work processes and a quantum improvement in the nature and flow of communications. Such a sophisticated system, incorporating data on the analytics of legal search engine results pages data, as well as the bounce rate per legal specialist, can now be used to help people in their web searches for answers to potential legal problems. Furthermore, the system synthesizes search terms to aid firms in the development of content that keeps them ahead of the competition. In doing so, client service can be bolstered, sectors eclipsed, and legal firms can thrive.

Pilot studies in legal firms suggest that searchers are more likely to go to a web page where they are offered a machine-generated answer over one where they are just offered a link. Most AI processing deals directly with individuals and their data, and often data subject to the common law, contractual obligations, and specific legislation. Protections are afforded clients in the common law. In order for lawyers to provide robust service delivery personalized to the client via these IT advances and hence meet their client's objectives, their data will need to be intersected. As in all data protection strategies, robust data and information governance will be necessary. This includes policies on retention and ultimately deleting unnecessary copies and references to that data and applying security controls proportionate to various recoverability scenarios following a notification from the client that they wish to exercise their rights. AI solutions case study Predictive analytics AI applications and interface AI risk assessment for client handling.

CHAPTER 6: AI TOOLS EVERY LAWYER SHOULD KNOW: FROM RESEARCH TO REVENUE

1. Evolution of AI in Legal Practice

In the past five years, AI has begun to transform key aspects of the legal profession. The transformation is happening against a backdrop of profound change in legal practice. Lawyers are operating in a global economy characterized by fierce competition, an exponential increase in the volume of business transactions, the emergence of new service delivery models, and a greater emphasis on specialization and quality. There are more lawyers competing for an expanding client base; clients increasingly demand more for less, and companies are consolidating their legal service providers. The migration of legal work provides both threats and opportunities to law firms, and the greatest barrier to law firm growth is the shortage of experienced, high-caliber practitioners. These characteristics of the legal profession are driving and legitimizing the development and implementation of AI tools. These challenges have had significant implications for law firms and have influenced legal practitioners to develop and deploy a set of information technology tools to streamline and modify legal practices. The legal profession has changed over time, different periods have observed different practices and different tools for the purpose of accomplishing legal work. AI is one such tool for legal practice in the twenty-first century that by anymeans will change the legal landscape in the near future, and lawyers have to keep themselves familiar with these changes, specially the seniors who their role is more about supervising juniors, if they can not keep the pace, definitely the Z generation will impress you with their findings and you will fail to understand the difference between an advice using an AI or HI (Human Intelligence).

2. Key AI Tools for Lawyers

Although AI and advanced computing will grow, models show rapid change in the legal profession, which is coming in the next few years. There are already different areas in which AI can assist and help lawyers and other law professionals, such as contract analysis and review, legal prediction, legal writing, intellectual property, due diligence, compliance, e-discovery, and clients' needs. This is the reason why different AI applications in law have focused on these areas or have started to appear in the market more or less quietly.

Contract Analysis: This is where AI has focused most of its potential so far. Several companies focus on AI technology for extraction and provide more detail. The markets with potential growth opportunities for legal services provided by technology, the number of lawyers that perform contract review tasks, focus on the entire contract. With the development of more complex technology, these forensic AI algorithms will understand the structure of the documents and the full combination possibilities in different ways. These platforms use assisted or automatic learning to create an intuitive interface, which allows the user to perform review tasks quickly, without requiring additional setup or programming. Some of the points that can be highlighted are the ability to customize searches based on keywords, entities, clauses, and other advanced functionalities.

2.1. LexisNexis

Lexis Research System database was designed to provide fast access to comprehensive legal research using a new concept: an online, intelligent legal research system employing interactive research between the area of the problem, the database, and the user. It is computer-assisted legal research. As such, it utilizes the features of the computer to assist the lawyer in performing research in a dramatically different way than is the case using non-technology-assisted means. The use of and the speed of research to which the lawyer has become accustomed with Lexis have already surpassed manually tenanted research libraries. Legal scholars and practitioners have become comfortable with the computer-assisted legal research within the turbocharged area of Lexis, which handles traditionally difficult tasks easily.

2.2. Westlaw Edge

Westlaw is a legal research service designed primarily for lawyers and legal professionals. It contains a database of law and case law, and other services that provide information such as news and current awareness services. As of 2019, Westlaw has 60 databases and 25 different research areas. Westlaw is a subscription-based service that allows users to access legal information. Westlaw has been described as the finest legal search engine available with a continued worldwide following. It has sometimes been described as being at the heart of legal innovation.

Westlaw Edge is an AI-driven legal research platform, and the addition of AI to the platform allows legal professionals to come to faster conclusions and recommendations on the basis of individual inferences drawn from common legally relevant texts. With the help of the WestSearch Plus function and the KeyCite Overruling Risk icons, Opposing Authority Signals, Case Summary, and the new legal writing tools, Westlaw Edge allows you to get better results and to work more efficiently without the stress of missing something hidden. With Westlaw Edge, legal professionals can more accurately and thoroughly look at their performance and evaluation on a particular matter and promote aspects that everybody values like time, precision, and defense strategies.

2.3. Ravel Law

2012 was also the year in which Nik Reed and Daniel Lewis founded a company that was then part of an accelerator program. Its mission is to innovate the legal research process by making it more user-friendly, intelligent, faster, and more productive. The company's product is a legal research tool that not only allows users to perform traditional text searches in a very user-friendly, fast, and simple way, but can also carry out much more advanced searches of documents. Thanks to the use of this tool, lawyers will have at their disposal a system that automatically creates visualizations, obtaining in this way, thanks to the ease that for many results may be difficult to obtain manually or through a traditional search system. The team's members include lawyers and software developers, alumni of the best universities.

From its beginnings, the company has chosen to use, as products of attraction, important cases in which the most famous judges were involved. It is thanks to this type of choice that many legal entities have started advertising technologically advanced tools, demonstrating how they can make access to justice easier, more immediate, and with considerable positive impacts not only on the work of the lawyer but also on that of the judges and, why not, of the entire judiciary. Not for nothing, in July 2017 the company received an important acknowledgment for its work, its acquisition by a major legal research company. The tool supports case law analysis by presenting the most cited case in case law together with visual representations, allowing the user to have an immediate overview of the trust received by each individual case.

2.4. *Relativity*

Relativity acquired the AI company Text IQ in January 2021. The proposed application for lawyers is to parse their document sets, identify not only where privileged or responsive information may reside, but also identify if this has raised concerns by employees upstream in the collection, review, analysis, or cognition process. The AI models developed by Text IQ to date include Resilience – measuring concern for mental health and wellness, Integrity – an anticipatory compliance tool, Etym – patient record insights, and Privilege – for document ranking. The fourth indicator of privilege leverages advanced encryption algorithms that run on-premise with "0-knowledge" so that none of the contents leave a firm's or client's control. Text IQ is already compatible with over 300 Document Management Systems, and the proprietary and unique resilience, compliance, and curiosity tools designed by Text IQ will require ethical judgment by lawyers and non-lawyers about their potential use and pitfalls, monitoring thresholds, and potential risk of overzealous deployment, which may lead to avoidable tensions and dispute challenges.

Relativity, much like iManage, has invested in the extended community model of allowing customers to easily access and add third-party applications, whether bespoke or preconfigured, to their SaaS or on-premise deployment. This also permits the lawyers involved to make use of additional AI tools or certified crowdsource tasks as outlined, inspecting the data that is created, updated, accessed, or addressed, powered by Relativity. The implemented AI appliances, as well as their operational controls, involved staff, debriefing, and the model that appears most prevalent, requires detailed planning and consideration from all practice disciplines and regions impacted. Highly functional AI, after all, if judged unethical or excessive, can be regulated against, so the reliance on and usability of a supportive AI ecosystem cannot be understated.

2.5. *Everlaw*

Everlaw is a powerful platform developed for managing huge amounts of data. Users are able to search, browse, and analyze data that might include some of the largest datasets, producing very fast results. The type of data uploaded to Everlaw may include multimedia, messages, and their attachments. Despite the substantial amount of these documents and various information, the produced analyses are done with high speed. There are a number of reasons and capabilities for using advanced machine learning and AI technology to create valuable legal intelligence that defines Everlaw users' experience. The mentioned AI capabilities are strongly supported by systems that generate automatic logging of who viewed what and when, and even create alerts when new material relevant to any particular existing investigation is uploaded by someone else. It is convenient to search using a combination of keywords as well as filters and even visual search filters that allow you to quickly mark or create facets based on the structural characteristics of the data.

Automatic document suggestions and findings are made by the software for complicated searches or entire sets of documents. Viewing, searching, and exporting the metadata in the dataroom are easy to manage due to the use of AI. Afterward, any search made for the information stored in the system may automatically change, since AI's suggestions can be used by the investigator to alter the search. To trace what steps were taken when investigating the datasets, all machine learning-powered results suggest why they were shown, and the theory behind these explanations is broken down for those currently using the data who are not experts in AI development.

2.6. Kira Systems

One might think that the digital age has indeed arrived when one learns that contracts can be read and understood efficiently and intelligently by computers. Yet, that is what the software Kira does. Kira was developed by a professional whose human rights and products liability work led to a venture into human rights in a more quantum sense. To evaluate these cases accurately, the developer found himself counting formally written genocide language in more than 2,000 pages of mostly fact witness testimony. "It was all so labor-intensive and unproductive," he said. "I used the development skills I acquired in my studies, bought some books on Boolean algebra, and set out to create a rudimentary expert system. It didn't have sophisticated natural language capabilities, but it saved a lot of time."

AI in Kira systems adds substantial value to the legal profession by offering a range of case and other content completion tools. This process involves machine contract reading of high-standard documents relating to the same matter without requiring a contract terms lexicon via the AI algorithm. With such help, the law firms' "best brains" can focus on actions that really require the best brains, the creation of sophisticated legal opinions that help clients' corporate goals favored by compliance.

2.7. Luminance

Luminance stands out in the field of LegalTech as an AI tool developed by lawyers and mathematicians. Trained by legal practitioners and mathematicians, the system was designed to work with complex contracts. It is claimed that Luminance can accurately seek the type of contract in which AI has the most potential for implementation, but the truth is that it can be used in other fields. Its strength lies in the speed of processing large volumes of contract data, including points related to the scope for amendment and other issues commonly appearing in due diligence processes, discrepancies, and missing obligations.

Non-lawyers can use their skills and eschew much of the work of contract review, often counting on a trial period that allows users to train the system according to their needs. The Luminance system also offers the possibility of cooperating with other tools in the field of due diligence and can be perfectly coordinated with other workflow management systems. Luminance applies principles from well-established areas of mathematics such as inductive logic and the Variational Bayes framework, which really allows the system to be instructed through the examples shown by various documents in the machine learning system and then possesses the logic of self-improvement when working.

2.8. LawGeex

LawGeex focuses on automating the review and approval of legal contracts in business, regarding transactional legal work. The service learns to analyze existing contract provisions to see if they are compliant with legal requirements as well as company policies and needs. Users input their company's preferences and risk tolerance, and the output is the instantaneous approval of the contract. LawGeex compares favorably in accuracy and speed. Instead of spending time reviewing and scanning contracts and avoiding mistakes in the process, the staff can do more productive work, thus increasing profits. However, it is hard to anticipate what kind of work firms will be transitioning to once contract reviewing is off their plate. It is important to note that contract drafting is not entirely automated; clients create the templates, which are then filled in by the software with user input. What is subjective and open to interpretation is taken care of by their legal team experts.

2.9. HotDocs

HotDocs is a tool for legal professionals to assist in document assembly. Legal documents often contain customized "blanks" or statewide options. Tools like HotDocs allow attorneys to collect all the necessary information from their clients, and then HotDocs uses that information to assemble the final document. This allows attorneys to generate documents much faster while reducing the risk of typos or mistakes. The cost of implementing HotDocs can be prohibitively high, but the return is often significant. This software is best integrated with larger law practices with significant document management needs.

HotDocs creates custom, transaction-ready documents using plain text templates that interview the end user to decide what terms to include. For example, when a HotDocs-enabled form template is opened, users are prompted to respond to a series of prompts and data entry forms that guide them through the document creation process. These entries are used to fill in the blanks and produce a finished document. The interview system it features is described to operate based on branching dialogues by limiting the logical disclosure of syntax that applies to information relevant to the context of particular responses. Some of the features that make it so successful for lawyers include the following.

2.10. Contract Express

Contract Express is a document automation tool that is well known in the legal industry. Its amazing ability to transform drafts into intelligent templates and generate prepopulated agreements has granted it widespread recognition all over the world. Highlighted features of the software include the one-time creation of templates, a separate clause bank with powerful security and rendering, excellent flexibility and management of questions, shortcuts, swift answers, a very clear Q&A interface, excellent customer support, a nifty proofreading gadget, hassle-free maintenance, and transparent price setting.

In summary, it is an application that has become famous for multiple reasons, the key being its speedy drafting. Whether your team is small or large, it is a popular choice to invest in and is seen as both cost and time-saving. Contract Express is a user-friendly document automation tool and is adept at turning your repetitive drafts into reusable templates, streamlining your document drafting process. Industry experts usually use it for services such as drafting, negotiation processes, and updating documents. Its innovative features indicate that an agreement can be approved and made actionable thanks to workflow. Its powerful market-tested technology also hints at it being one of the leaders in software choice for legal professionals.

2.11. Clio

Clio, a legal tech company based in Canada, offers a suite of software solutions for managing various aspects of a legal practice. Derived from the ancient Greek goddess of history, Clio is a cloud-based case management, time tracking, and legal billing application designed to provide lawyers with a secure, mobile, online platform. The solution is built around optimizing the functions of legal business in different areas, including administrative tasks. Besides, Clio CRM's objective is to address the potential problems of storing fund accounts, productivity, and client retention solutions in law firms. Using Clio helps to track client communications and documents, especially when there is a high inbound stream.

The software allows for the automatic capture of every phone call, email, or meeting directly to your case files, converting tracked time into comprehensive reports, managing access and permissions, and integrating with third-party applications. Clio's API is open and licensed. The company runs a developer program that permits any developer to access all matters, create, and operate at their fingertips to develop new integrations. With Clio, lawyers can easily share with clients what they need, when they need it. After the attorney has found the client, the Rights Management Platform provides clients with additional secure access and allows them to enter and order the document to file. Clio helps law firms manage and control secured systems and protects them from interventions that may violate the privilege rights of clients.

2.12. PracticePanther

PracticePanther was established as a useful tool to assist legal professionals in managing their practice. It was created to offer an effective tool that would not only allow staff to swipe and sign up clients quickly and efficiently but also provide interactive tools that could help them automate workflows, create customizable templates for different needs in a legal practice, and track real activities. To help lawyers build trust with their clients, practitioners also have the ability to securely share data. To connect these professional capabilities with their client base, PracticePanther recognizes that innovation is highly important and is always looking forward to developing faster and easier solutions. Established in 2012, by the end of 2020, PracticePanther had taken lessons and improved its service to the extent of providing lawyers with over 1,000 pre-designed automated documents that can instantly be adjusted to the unique needs of a law practice. It has also been integrated with e-signature tools to allow document signing without the need for printing or scanning, and other features include time capture enhancements, document processing, a roster of personalized tools, personalized assistance, comprehensive organizational aids, and mobile accessibility. Complete reliability with comprehensive functionality, adequate versatility, and reasonable prices prompted many lawyers to heavily deploy PracticePanther and accept its satisfactory output.

2.13. Premonition

It is a record of a presentation by the CEO of a big data platform that monetizes legal data by building predictive models. The CEO was the first female Country Manager of an investment bank in the 1980s. When she left a couple of years ago, women ran 12 of them. "I thought it was normal," she says, "but it seems I was a harbinger of the circle of death. That's the mortality of innovation in any industry; once it loses gender diversity, the gender-diverse people have left. Leaders don't notice because it was just normal to them too.

About 173 people graduate from law school every year in the US, and four have jobs. The goal is to be the Bloomberg of the legal profession and to break that circle of innovation. They make money by selling data to companies that will use it to inform legal strategy and through doing early case assessments to make predictions about the outcome. They understand that if we could forecast whether a judge, lawyer, or party will end well or poorly before we engage, many disputes would dissolve before they begin. For that reason, they concentrate all of their efforts on using heavy artificial intelligence to predict. They believe that for the legal analytics segment of the legal industry to grow, it is paramount to understand that it is not counting wins. They need to determine whether somebody is better than the client or not.

2.14. Juris-Metrics

A legal scientific research area analyzes whether judicial behavior can be quantified, measured, and modeled. Juris-Metrics integrates methodologies for detecting weaknesses and strengths of legal systems, such as modeling how and why legal outcomes change, improving law's predictive functions, while systematizing the recording processes of judicial activities. Beneficiary tools: The research area is exploited by research scholars and interested stakeholders with tools tailored to keep score of judicial decisions and activities in a structured electronic Labour Tutor combined with databases, such as a repository of judicial behaviors being developed. Findings on natural language processing are tailored for semantical analyses. Case-law databases and semantic legal data. Recent results: The model has been empirically validated to provide an unbiased account for juridical scores, without contributing to the abusive use of judicial practice prediction by special interest groups. The expected use declines information asymmetry in judicial scoring processes. Providing greater transparency of judicial performance metrics, the research aim is to balance the demand for the accountability of legal systems and the judges' profession with the freedom of interpretative judicial activity and the separation of judicial powers.

2.15. DoNotPay

With $1.1M from Andreessen, DoNotPay launches 1,000 new bots to help you with your legal problems. DoNotPay is an interactive robot assistant for legal services, including an AI tool programmed one year ago to help drivers contest parking tickets and cover legal issues in non-English speaking environments. Another U.S. tool helps low-income people make a claim against their landlord. Joshua Browder, the founder and CEO of DoNotPay, says that 160,000 parking tickets have been contested, totaling 3 million U.S. dollars. The normal error of parking meters is 35%. There are many talented lawyers, but with the help of robots, they can use their expertise for the benefit of society. One of the principal risks is the general mistrust of AI and the unavailability of AI for law graduates from the university. However, DoNotPay seems to increase philanthropic legal services for the benefit of society.

The term "DoNotPay" was purposely chosen by Josh Browder to highlight that the nascent AI sector is not offering enough philanthropic AI services. One of the reasons to focus on parking tickets at the beginning of DoNotPay was that it cannot be perceived negatively compared to the old "nasty" Arnold, who is now socialized by the parking meter error. Most cases, in Josh Browder's opinion, are unfair, like those of large groups of people of African American origin who have received multiple fines. The government tends to avoid AI to solve their social problems, although all the necessary data are available. There is a U.S. legal provision allowing people to invent new ways to interpret the law if the new application of law prevents actual government responsibility by reducing prison violations. It is like the "Robin Hood Law" for the benefit of society. This AI is a "Robin Hood" model of negatively perceived legal scripts or codes, which are instead legally accepted in the interest of society.

2.16. Ross Intelligence

Although AI does show promise, its current real-world applications in the law have been found to have limitations and efficacy issues. AI legal engines that serve as legal research assistant tools have been discovered to provide disappointing and sometimes incorrect search results, and sometimes the results have been non-responsive. Although AI can parse data more efficiently than human beings by extracting relevant data patterns from large databases without requiring litigation discovery, AI has limitations in interpreting contracts in vague and creative ways as would be necessary in business settings. AI has problems with dealing with the law in a non-legally regulated manner. Statistical-based AI designs find it difficult to predict when the legislature has been abusive or when the case law growth cycle is approaching its natural endpoint. AI depends on the data and the algorithms. The presence of incomplete or biased data or poorly designed algorithms can lead to incorrect human bias. Furthermore, AI tools that predict case outcomes, for the most part, have not been optimized for broader, more general usage.

Legal search and document assembly are obvious first targets because the client directly stands to save fees by reducing relevant attorney time. Other areas, such as legal format document stores, would possibly require a networked and portable device, but there is the implicit promise that such tools will reduce the need for tactical spending. The AI legal assistant has distinguished itself by providing better search algorithms. Among the many cases cited are instances where other rival AI tools returned inappropriate or irrelevant materials because they utilized metrics that were too simple, which inadvertently returned irrelevant or promotional results instead of the desired data. The technique relies on a complex, multi-featured neural net representative, iterative machine learning-based method of keyword-based and machine learning-based ranking of entries. Only natural language legal search engines incorporate the use of natural language generation components. Unlike the other tools, it also tries to understand what actions the client intends to take in a dialog format. With regard to legal document stores, it does not just have basic documents—it also allows the client to generate a document as a PDF as well as a companion Word document that contains variables and defaults that can be manually fine-tuned by the client.

2.17. ChatGPT

ChatGPT is a state-of-the-art large language model that can engage in casual conversation. It has the ability to generate human-like text based on its input and can even provide reasonable answers to prompts. As chatbots can handle simple tasks, they can often be used in customer service jobs to handle complaints by guiding customers through forms, information requests, and other tasks. However, its complexity can be tuned to generate very detailed responses. ChatGPT has a smaller language model, with 117 million parameters and a capability to generate acceptable responses for general conversation. Additionally, special-purpose language models can address specific issues in various topics, including law.

For conversational AI systems, several successful language models have been introduced. Attention is one of the most common components in these types of models. The BERT model was the first praxis to be utilized. It operates as an attention-based mechanism, capable of generating only a one-way context window. The predecessor of GPT is the first bidirectional sequence transformer model to utilize an attention mechanism in a generative context, originated from a unidirectional language model. Besides, the language modelling approach used in GPT-2 is also distinguished. The unidirectional nature of long-form text generation is indeed a critical flaw in ChatGPT. The context that GPT-2 receives is by pre-pending supplied text to the prompts. ChatGPT models a bi-directional context by concatenating the query to the context, which is the correct attachment method.

ChatGPT is not a legal based platform yet, however the machine learning can be incredibly seen as it can change to any platform according to your needs, but from my own perspective you cannot rely on its outcome yet as a legal platform, you can rephrase or understand certain paragraph or clause by asking the AI to simplify them make it is easy to absorb, but I am afraid having a legal clause or reviewing a contract could be something that you can depend on in the current being, using it for such mentioned purposes could be acceptable.

2.18. TimeSolv

TimeSolv can be considered one of the most typical time tracking programs available on the market, even today. It is particularly designed for lawyers and is a web-based program that they can access anywhere in the world online. TimeSolv allows its users to enter a description of their work, the billable time, and any cost rate. TimeSolv converts this information into the format of a billing report that can be printed on letterhead to be sent to the client.

Additional software is not needed to create an invoice; therefore, it does not require any further office software. TimeSolv also has a monthly subscription fee for either the standard or law office edition. TimeSolv can be used to keep track of time from the office, from one's home, or from a remote location. It can provide up-to-date information on the status of a client's case.

The program also allows for employee hierarchy: that is, attorneys, who typically have an hourly rate, law clerks, paralegals, support staff, and part-time staff can all be assigned different billing rates. Therefore, this program allows law offices to keep electronic time sheets to calculate individual performance, productivity, accuracy, and corresponding compensation customized to varied employee roles and responsibilities. The office search for work (who is doing what: jobs and costs), billing, documenting, and customer support are also accelerated due to all pre-scheduled results. Its benefits include efficient account administration in reducing the time and money necessary for workers' manual billing of company accounts.

2.19. Zola Suite

Lawyers are constantly on the move, and the resources of the firms in which they work need to move with them. Zola Suite is a legal practice management and legal billing software designed for legal professionals who are tech-savvy and forward-thinking. This software combines an innovative approach with a combination of technology. It offers tools for contacts, events, documents, and email. As a legal document management system, Zola Suite provides users with a complete and intuitive structure to arrange access to documents and emails in a safe way. Moreover, Zola Suite provides the ability to automate legal billing through the publication of differing laws. This legal billing software for lawyers is flexible and allows for relatively cost-effective billing. Zola Suite can display records and documents related to connections, events, cases, discoveries, invoices, associations, checks, registrations, credit cards, expenses, time costs, appointments, and target events. This cloud-based platform is widely integrated with essential applications for legal experts and is efficient and time-saving. You are enabled by this firm from anywhere, at any time, on any device.

2.20. Icertis

Icertis provides a contract management platform in the cloud, which is a hit with legal department staff, contract managers, and procurement professionals alike. The notion that the general counsel position has to evolve and provide input into making the entire corporation become more risk-averse and regulation-compliant is taking firm root both outside the United States and among countries with market-based economies. Globalization and the shift from an industrial to a knowledge economy are flattening corporate organizations.

Its attractive and modern user interface increases user adoption across an enterprise, and early upgrades and excellent customer support, with control by competent senior management, contribute to strong customer retention. Its deployment times and ease of customization reduce the burden on IT, accelerate projects, and demonstrably save on project costs. Icertis also burnished its reputation for stellar customer satisfaction. Its performance, executive chain of command, technology differentiation, the strength of partnerships, and existing market influence are visible in a mature and disciplined execution team capable of steady growth.

2.21. DocuSign CLM

DocuSign CLM (Contract Lifecycle Management) is designed to help organizations accelerate their contract cycle times, enabling compliance and enhancing job satisfaction. The DocuSign CLM ecosystem provides users with the ability to manage contracts and agreements. Through the integration with tools, the system becomes a central repository of all related data. The benefits of these integrations with software commonly used by lawyers are usually defined by the possibility of having all the business's lifecycle data in one single place. The most valuable feature is the AI for contract analysis, which could mitigate the risks of possible errors in the contracting process, ensure compliance, and automatically fill potential risks and obligations to be managed during operations. All representatives of the organization are required to use the rules and clauses developed by lawyers or with legal expertise.

It could also hasten the electronic payment requests for completion, automate the compliance checks, and manage the task of saving and keeping the documents safe in the indexing process. The work of the legal department will finally create value for the business. The purchase requests from the departments are easy to read and evaluate when the lawyer defines and classifies the type of obligation targeted at its functions. The software assigns automatic copies to the areas of the company defined at the time of configuration, providing assistance in the operation for the checks that in the past have been done manually by the legal department or that have been missed with dire consequences for the business.

2.22. Casetext

Casetext is built to save lawyers time by giving them instant access to the research of other attorneys so they can more effectively analyze cases, write briefs, and have informed conversations with clients. It does this by building the most comprehensive database of case law available, offered at a variety of price points and licensing plans. Casetext also has a tool that compares a brief to millions of other court documents, helping lawyers find relevant case law and arguments in a single click. With a smart price and a reasonable price point, Casetext takes a step back by making case law more affordable and breaks down barriers for new law firms to provide for their clients. To date, Casetext has served more than 500,000 lawyers in over 30 countries and has been trusted by more than 4,500 law firms, governments, and organizations to address their primary legal research needs. These include large firms, tax firms, and public entities. In 2010, Casetext was co-founded by law student Jake Heller and software programmer Pablo Arredondo in Stanford. Since then, the Casetext team has expanded to include data scientists, designers, and other legal experts dedicated to future-proofing Casetext's system to serve the modern practice and lawyers' future legal needs as well.

2.23. Blue J Legal

Blue J Legal is founded by a father-son duo with impressive credentials. Their AI tool Tax Foresight is specifically designed for tax lawyers. Blue J uses the predictive and analytical capabilities of AI to let legal professionals find answers to the most critical legal matters. The main purpose of Blue J Legal is to help lawyers predict legal outcomes when the law lacks sufficient clarity. With the help of the tools provided by Blue J, law firms can easily gather data and understand how the law works, and then apply that understanding to assist clients. Blue J has come in handy for tax lawyers, as it not only assists in making predictions about how the courts are likely to interpret the law on a specific legal issue, but also presents a detailed analysis of how the AI system reached its conclusions. Choose and streamline your benefits with this one-of-a-kind AI tool.

2.24. Diligent

One of the key tasks NDA professionals perform is the analysis of a variety of interesting issues. However, the tools that are normally used in process may not be easy to find or in place for the language pair/topic required. This section presents a tool that partially automates the creation of corpora by extracting sentences related to a specific topic from an arbitrary set of documents. This capability can be of interest not only for translators and students, but also professionals interested in enhancing this type of analysis-based deliverable and researchers interested in other kinds of textual information extraction. The tool has been programmed using a high-level programming language known for its data-manipulation capabilities. It also uses some free software tools that could be used for other purposes. The remaining sections of the document present the technical and resource requirements and features of the tool to help determine its usefulness and applicability to different types of issues.

2.25. eBrevia

This is a specialized tool developed with the aim of suggesting contracts and their parts to lawyers, based on the content analysis of a training corpus properly classified by a group of experts. Unlike traditional contract generation tools, it does not require human training to manifest patterns, but learns by example, based on textual and visual context. To this end, it is driven by a reinforcement learning system that starts from a verb and remains uncertain about the meaning of the following content until the entire extracted text can be analyzed. Finally, it is designed to operate on unknown text without sacrificing accuracy.

This toolkit is noted to be very useful for both legal researchers and practitioners, who can search for the clauses in the documents and thus speed up reading time. Nevertheless, it is a training tool that requires a significant amount of data to begin operating at decent accuracies, particularly within small niches and industry-specific areas with a unique driving language. It should be noted, in this context, that when using this type of technology as a lawyer, the duty of confidentiality is an issue.

2.26. ClauseMatch

ClauseMatch is a smart document collaboration platform with comparison engines that enable comparison as you type and a side-by-side comparison view, seamlessly embedded into Word. The platform allows all types of documents spanning across different business units not only to compare and match but also to collaborate on a single document. The comparison engines are powered by AI and machine learning to assist general counsels, chief compliance officers, chief risk officers, and other professionals at financial institutions, broker-dealers, investment advisers, asset management, insurance, consumer goods companies, and many other industries. ClauseMatch is a single source of truth currently used for policies and procedures, guidelines and manuals, regulations, contract repositories, and financial documents, promising to revolutionize the way people work to make day-to-day business routines more efficient. The platform is currently used by buy-side transaction documentation teams for collaboration and management of document projects and by compliance for policies and procedures alongside the compliance mapping engine with machine-learning capability to automate regulatory obligations mapping. It also solves issues naturally listed with the redlining process being complicated and time-consuming, requirements of collaboration and comments being ranged, and, of course, never-ending disputes. The platform is built to become an integrated workflow solution having core features for live, streamlined, and checked amendments of documents, as well as root-cause analysis for auditing and reporting, and audit trails to provide a history of the process. ClauseMatch presents a good alternative to industry pairs because it offers a true SaaS solution without on-premise installation with several plugins to integrate applications for easy billable user management and document repository access.

2.27. ComplyAdvantage

ComplyAdvantage's AI-enhanced machine learning tool suite provides a cutting-edge solution to combat money laundering and enhance anti-money laundering compliance programs. The sanctions service enables firms to check client information against national and international sanctions lists in real time, thus enabling firms to prevent and deter individuals engaging in fraud and criminal activities as per their AML policies. The technology processes diverse types of information with a high level of accuracy. ComplyAdvantage's sophisticated AML tool connects authoritative sanctions lists and regulatory releases in a structured manner to provide connected information for each registered entity to identify risks, verify risk information, and general information regarding countries and the scope of activities performed within these countries.

ComplyAdvantage's other AML tool, the Adverse Information tool, connects critics from news sources and public records databases to provide an integral data source for collusion checks for registered entities. It enables the detection of politically exposed individuals or their relations, and other risks for anti-corruption compliance policy. The technology connects alternative information to authoritative sources and has a high level of accuracy. Furthermore, it also connects information regarding politically exposed individuals and their connections, and a vast array of estate information, including mass leaks of data, from diverse primary documents. These documents include media, market services, real property registers, business records, and other reliable public records. The tool detects and verifies risk and general information regarding countries and the scope of business activities performed in these countries. This is done by assessing and providing an accurate and individualized level of service to each registered entity.

2.28. iManage

One such legal tech provider is iManage. iManage is the leader in managing the culture of work for law firms, corporations, financial services, and more. It promotes digital transformation and helps organizations leverage the right knowledge and insights to improve client services and add more value. Their solutions offer an open, secure, and extensible document and email management collaboration platform. It helps to reduce the cost of risk connected with legal disputes and regulatory challenges. In addition, it modernizes legal, corporate, real estate, public sector, and many other headquarters, providing the necessary outcome. Its AI-enhanced solution allows companies to take business value from data and interact across processes, people, and systems. Within law firms, several specialized products were developed to support the broader iManage Work 10, providing legal-specific features within the same platform, such as document automation portals, key presentation spreading, automatic surfacing of relevant information governing novel issues, extranets, the ability to tightly control documents and prevent data breaches, and the option to effectively ensure your documents are delivered exactly the way you need them, along with other functions. Their RAVN module is commonly used for filing, knowledge management strategy guidance, customized extranets, query spending inclusion algorithms analysis, self-service QA inquiries, organizing instantaneous legal department portals, legal project operations, and BI graph generation.

2.29. Clarivate

NLP engines and ML can be used to extract automation or to create insights. For the legal professional, automated citation checks are popular tools in document review, for their generation of reports and in the task of proving originality did not overcome Section 67 of the Copyright Act. The platform is able to authenticate the originality of publications. It serves as a lookout point for several publishers, and some judges, especially in copyright cases, require that this stage be completed as proof of authentication of the content generated by these tools.

Many judges, upon requesting a survey of the plaintiff's publications, order the subscription to the tool. There is still a small percentage of cases that prefer another query. On the other hand, the concept of disseminating secondary or high-quality legal content has not been widely explored. Some articles are part of a vast content collection. Unlike another product, they allow the user to consult some documents without technical limitations, without quotas for sharing within their office or among lawyers of the same law firm. The platform covers relevant publishers, but the cost is high. Their subscriptions focus on academic, corporate, or specific needs.

2.30. Anaqua

Anaqua is a Boston-based company that has developed patent management software. The company works in a rather specialized niche, serving everyone involved in the intense patent battlefields. This means the system is as much geared for law firms as it is for inventors and big corporations seeking intellectual property assets. Among its services, Anaqua simplifies the streamlining of the big IP tasks, including the management of the portfolio, the protection of the innovation, and the proper guidance of the strategy. They offer an enterprise patent management system designed to help companies use a single platform so that they can globally execute their patent strategy. Possible customers can be found among corporations, corporate law firms, and research companies in all areas such as pharmaceuticals, computer services, electronics, biotechnology, medical devices, and chemicals. Anaqua's system is imbued with artificial intelligence technology and strong reporting to meet the growing business demands of several, enabled by the company's notoriety in combining intellectual property information and lifelike workflows. Their partners are interested in increasing innovation. But it is the vast amount of data that increases the company's interest in increasing knowledge about patented assets, how they compare, and what is relevant. Their enterprise-class patent management software is used by many corporations in addition to more than 15,000 other users in hundreds of companies around the world.

2.31. Canva

The promise of Canva for any professional to create their material of any kind using an integrated user-friendly system is just impressive! The Canva platform is not only user-friendly, but it can also provide publication material that is Instagram or Pinterest worthy. Canva takes the design—whether it is inspirational quotes, banners, or book covers—to another level altogether, with the user being able to design their own material that could require the skills of a graphic designer! Of course, being able to design one's own business card or the material that is going to be used to make an Instagram connection with a judge might be of the desired level for a law student, but it might not even be a secondary skill required of a practicing lawyer.

Visual displays of information are always impressive, as is displaying information in such an interesting way that makes people read the content. Visual representations are also an alternate aid to the verbal aspect of communicating information. Thus, whether it is a PowerPoint required to present information in an interesting way in court or a poster required for an outreach program, with the library of templates and the ability to create one's own design offered by Canva, users can have striking visual displays of information.

3. Applications and Use Cases

A key issue in a tech-embedded approach is determining how AI and other intelligent analysis tools can improve processes and functionalities. There are many targets to aim at. AI has established promising paths by exclusively solving problems that have always sustained the consideration of lawyers, such as concept classification, document analysis, filtering, prioritization, summarization, abstraction, customization, translation, interpretation, predictive tactics, and inference. It has been used in various areas, from improving the prediction of case trial results and their potential to affect contracts or transactions to designing dynamic reconfigurable legislative regulations.

The array of tools and applications suggested for lawyers keeps increasing. Advanced search functions appear to be a basic feature. AI technology helps to improve traditional search tools and enhances access to resources with search context options, including syntax recognition, as well as drill-down filters, taxonomy, and user-defined templates. Moreover, AI integrated into the search function may also provide results that incorporate questions about concepts by recognizing relations between cases, documents, or regulations. These questions of intermediate limits could also be answered by comparing the fragments of cases provided by the system and can also infer recommendations for the outsourcing and reference of internal preparation.

3.1. *Legal Research and Case Analysis*

AI can be a valuable ally in the field of legal research and case analysis. It allows lawyers to access an immense amount of legal information that would be impossible to study in a human lifetime and analyze it in ways that humans could never do unaided. The development of AI systems for legal research is nothing new; in fact, it has a history of more than 30 years. Nevertheless, the current state of the art in natural language processing and machine learning systems have made legal research AI the most important trend in the field. The best AI legal research tools use natural language processing to allow questions and answers in natural language and comprehend sophisticated concepts. These technologies make them powerful tools for fast, precise, and insightful results. The use of case law and legal research engines will make some services in current legal departments using paralegals unnecessary or will allow the legal departments to incorporate them with little added cost, which may help to decrease the high cost that this area historically presents.

AI legal research tools search through vast amounts of cases, statutes, and regulations, understanding complex questions in natural language and providing very accurate results in a fraction of the time needed for a human to do it. With the use of these legal research tools, consumers and small firms may access the same information that major sophisticated law firms have, leveling the field. Furthermore, simple visualization techniques will allow these users to benefit from insights derived from access to big legal data. With these types of tools, we could visualize how different judges have ruled on similar cases or how often certain judges have ruled in certain ways, helping lawyers to evaluate the potential success of a case or to anticipate the behavior of a specific judge. These AI-powered research platforms already have some predictive capacity: to understand the possible outcome and the reasons that led to it. These types of AI tools can help with due diligence procedures for M&A deals, real estate, or in any other search where a massive use of legal documentation is required.

3.2. *Contract Review and Management*

With respect to the contractual relationships that are encompassed by entity management in the broadest context possible, the inclusion of contracts as part of entity management is readily apparent. Other than the company constitution, which defines certain relationships and how the company will act, the governing legislation and regulations, and the shareholders' agreements that deal with operations and sorting out disputes between the shareholders, and a business plan, contracts are the glue that holds an organization together, ensuring that the trust inherent in the human interactions concerning limited companies is respected and upheld. Hence, it is hardly surprising that lawyers, particularly those operating within the in-house legal environment, are keen to undertake a review of any kind of commercial contracts regularly entered into by the business to ascertain the rights and obligations that may exist. The review process is beneficial for a number of reasons, with this knowledge helping minimize the potential exposure incurred by the business and contributing to enhancing its business activities that are beneficial. Judicious management of the contractual relationships is critical. Editorial assistance by artificial intelligence tools, from simple clause checking processes, which operate only to see if pre-defined terms are included, to more complex contract analysis tools, which can help ensure that the contract is properly compliant with pre-established standards, may be both a time and money saver as well as a risk management exercise.

3.3. Due Diligence and Compliance

AI-powered platforms can read and understand documents related to financial, tax, or legal aspects of a company's business. Thus, AI can help companies and investors during M&A transactions, more efficiently identify companies with problematic compliance history, speed up business decisions, and thus lower costs. M&A deal flow often encompasses repetitive manual tasks related to administrative, financial, legal, tax, and IT due diligence processes. These tasks are relatively time-consuming, at least when done professionally. Thus, innovation that can save man-hours is always wanted. AI models can aid company lawyers, outsiders who are providing due diligence support, or experts who are hired for a smaller span of time.

AI models can also read data to discover noncompliance situations. AI also provides tools that allow management to monitor, respond to, and prevent risks; accordingly, more and more businesses are planning to spend on legal management software. The market for business legal software will see significant growth. The market demand for legal technology is unprecedented. Even before the leadership of technology sparked mass awareness, the market for such applications is expected to continue to expand significantly. Every software that helps companies maintain compliance with the new requirements is going to find jobs. What is the story, then? The story, as we argue, is due to a new generation of legal technology startups that serve a significant portion of the venture market. These players focus on three key areas that businesses pay attention to: understanding and complying with new consumer protections, developing and maintaining robust privacy and data security policies and procedures, and creating value for consumers.

3.4. *Document Automation and Assembly*

Document automation is a specific term recognized and promoted by document automation programs. These products automate the process of creating templates that are then used by the computer to create complex documents. In the legal profession, where form documents are very prevalent, type 1 document automation is likely to have a significant impact. Document assembly, also known as document assembly systems, was one of the first forms of intelligent software on the market. The first time a document assembly program was ever used in the legal profession, the impact it had was so high that most attorneys have since that time come to believe that the use of document assembly significantly improves their productivity, professionalism, and efficiency.

Some documents, such as wills or contracts, can be extremely complex and voluminous, containing numerous standard paragraphs with numerous permutations that are inserted or omitted, depending on the requirements of the individual case. The system not only assembles final documents from appropriate standard text, but also permits users to draft complex documents simply by entering the basic data, leaving word handling chores to the computer. Program development became feasible only when advances in artificial intelligence assisted in providing computers with the capability to recognize textual patterns, grammatical structures, and combinations of words that convey meanings. With the incorporation of knowledge-driven reasoning, the development of document assembly systems could safely progress so that the machines could complete tasks previously performed by streamliners.

3.5. *Predictive Analytics and Decision Support*

Predictive analysis is the technique that uses data to make predictions about the future, in particular by connecting to big data processing and machine learning capabilities. Predictive analytics often spreads to all functions of the legal department, such as legal, compliance, intellectual property, and others. With the help of machine learning workflows, predictive analytics is becoming increasingly important as the focus of lawyers' analysis moves from the "what" in the data to the "so what". This is not about the development of predictions – it's mostly about the development of insights, predictions, and suggestions that are critical to a company's success or survival. In the eyes of macro-organizations, the role and function of the in-house lawyer are changing, integrating and fusing traditional legal services into the business services pipeline. Delivering a machine learning model to demonstrate the thought process required to dispose of the predictive legal data will make the added value of lawyers more evident. The commission rate will increasingly reflect this.

Organizing and assigning the right work to the right staff while transmitting domain knowledge are critical barriers to entry in machine learning projects. Another thing is that not everything can be bought, but there are good chances of limited benefit from in-sourcing, or only a weak hit on the law firm's confidentiality obligations. This will provide some strategies to overcome these key challenges. The key to the future operation of this technology, like many domain knowledge and transformational technologies, is to ensure that new AI investments are firmly tied to the business's current and future goals, including the relationship between lawyers in the company and the CIO. Prediction is by far the most common legal use case for machine learning. Seasoned legal professionals, who specialize in providing executive coaching, business consulting, economic investigation, and litigation support, manage large e-discovery projects and demonstrate the value of the new technology for the company they are trying to serve.

4. Impact of AI on the Legal Profession

So, what is the impact of artificial intelligence on the legal profession? Probably the most common impression lawyers have of AI is the impact it will have on the demand for legal services. It is stated that the growing adoption of AI in discovery and due diligence could negatively impact paralegals and associates who have traditionally been the ones to review and compile documents. It is asserted that AI could eliminate a significant number of legal jobs a year. It is argued that the ratio of paralegals and legal office support personnel employed by the major law firms has reduced more than 16 percent between 2013 and 2018, and will further reduce by more than 26 percent by 2023. Nevertheless, a balanced picture is presented. In education, it is observed that current AI applications would cause traditional legal education to be smaller and less expensive. For the practice of law, it is asserted that it could eliminate rote tasks and spur demand for more qualitative work. It is suggested that this would free attorneys from their current systems to carry on more valuable tasks.

Although different opinions do exist in predicting the impact of AI on the legal industry, it is obvious that the future of the legal industry landscape will be considered along with the change of the legal workspace. The business model of most law firms is based on the criminalization of work on a timesheet that relies heavily on the billable hour. It is long known that this model produces misalignments between what law firms sell and what clients buy. In reality, many clients want the service that was promised more than that of per hour, so that charging this way has attracted significant criticism. AI may have the potential to mitigate this criticism. Of course, AI can also impact the organizational structure of a law firm in many ways. This includes business organization, association with other non-legal advisors, the combination of legal groups, management, new processes of preference, and the training of lawyers.

4.1. *Efficiency and Productivity*

The primary and most immediately recognized impact of implementing AI tools in the legal sector is the potential to significantly enhance efficiency and improve productivity. This increased efficiency is largely owing to these tools' abilities to process large volumes of data, understand complex legal material, learn from history, and deduce outcomes from given facts. Efficiency and productivity within the legal profession unquestionably have associated monetary benefits for individual lawyers and legal providers. However, experts are concerned that the introduction of AI will eliminate too many jobs and lead to too few people gaining access to justice. The productivity of the courts can also face a tremendous strain as a result of greater numbers of hearings required to resolve disputes that AI alone was unable to handle. With the large numbers of cases currently being won or settled without the legal process and in the absence of legal advice, it is easy to bypass the courts. The legal industry has for many years been criticized for its lack of progress in increasing productivity compared to other sectors. The factual reasons for this are plentiful and complex. However, the nature of the industry itself, for example, its heavy reliance on legal skills, its sole possession of bespoke or specialized information, its several opposing incentives that discourage efficiency-increasing initiatives, and its historic, inherited operating models are contributing factors. AI is equipped to revolutionize the legal industry by enabling the legal profession to operate more on par with other sectors in the following ways: by becoming adept at processing data, recognizing patterns, understanding natural language, identifying events and relationships, handling complex outcomes, making decisions, and fully automating specific tasks, activities, and processes. These functionalities lead to increased efficiency and reduce the extent of human involvement within legal tasks.

4.2. *Cost Reduction and Time Savings*

Cost reduction and time savings are two highly significant effects of introducing AI in the legal profession. Today's legal services market comprises cost-sensitive clients, so firms that demonstrate cost reduction offer tremendous value. This embodiment of value makes maintaining and attracting clients a simple process for the introducing firms. By sharing significant cost reduction benefits with clients, firms also deliver immediate economic insurance for their clients. If and when the impact is achieved, the results give firms the ability to command more client-responsive legal fees. At this stage, firms do not have to constantly project revenues from a number of billable hours into the future. For certain businesses, they may not charge their clients an hourly fee at all. This fixed-price or fee model also offers the benefit of reliable budgeting for legal services, as the company knows exactly how much they will have to pay when they hire a lawyer.

The use of knowledge management systems leads to time savings in the production phase as well. Lawyers can adjust their actions to suit their activities in the pursuit of skills-based tasks or better client relationships with more decision-supportive tasks and the acquisition of business knowledge. Having the necessary materials available increases efficiency while performing tasks, resulting in more accurate work. In particular, this means that the time it takes to solve specific problems and access material is reduced considerably. Many law firms that have implemented legal process improvement techniques have saved a significant amount of time by reducing the number of times it takes to search for and file documents. The commercial legal management service model then begins to replicate a similar approach to what has been done successfully with legal consulting, management, and information services.

4.3. Enhanced Accuracy and Consistency

One main area where using AI tools can significantly enhance lawyering is by improving the accuracy and consistency of legal services. Accuracy is a core competency in the practice of law. The essence of practicing law is to accomplish results that are both legally and factually correct, all else being equal. Yet, ensuring the accuracy of legal work is an increasingly challenging task. This is because the volume and complexity of legal information—encompassing statutes, regulations, case law, and negotiated documents—are far too great for any human being to process without the help of machines. Ensuring the accuracy of legal research is essential—so much so, in fact, that lawyers are legally required to do the best possible job. The Model Rules require that "a lawyer shall provide competent representation to a client," and "competent representation" is defined as one where the lawyer "possesses the legal knowledge, skill, thoroughness, and preparation reasonably necessary for the representation."

4.4. Improved Client Service and Satisfaction

The advance of AI technology at a breathtaking speed improves legal services by assisting lawyers with more precise legal advice, faster, and with lower costs, ultimately leading to increased client satisfaction and loyalty. By using AI, e-discovery can be performed in matters that previously might not have had the resources to justify e-discovery, making it possible to provide a higher quality of legal representation. Since AI can perform repetitive tasks quickly, accurately, and efficiently, it enhances transparency and client satisfaction by allowing an optional level of decision-making on a cost basis. Additionally, AI can help firms deliver more data-driven client advice and solutions that clients can use in-house, enhancing client service. AI also enhances the capabilities of the entire workforce in a law firm, making it easier for junior lawyers to conduct research, put together facts, and prepare straightforward pleadings and briefs in routine matters. Delegating repetitive legal work to diligently designed and novel AI decreases the chances of human errors, accelerates the decision-making process, and provides the highest level of support and customer satisfaction by firmly promoting the legal profession in the long term. By implementing AI software, lawyers can immediately and accurately advise their clients on a wide variety of legal matters. Mimicking the information-gathering techniques of an army of human paralegals, AI software can quickly produce massive volumes of discovery documents to advise whether given patent documents would be printed prior to or stopped from issuance if they were found to lack the vital information. With a labor supply that never tires and charges nothing to work, AI comprises an inexpensive tool to support the depositions of the profound.

4.5. Ethical and Regulatory Considerations

Whether driven by practitioner self-regulation or broader ethical considerations, the delivery of legal services entails distinct notions that are designed to support individual lawyers or their clients. These principal principles include the obligation of confidentiality, protection from the self-interest of lawyers, absolute loyalty, client autonomy, the unauthorized sharing of fees, and good faith. We introduce and explain these principles and other provisions proposed in the Model Code, the main specifications proposed by the associations that regulate the profession, and the principles developed by the General Council of the Spanish Lawyers. Finally, concrete recommendations are provided on improving the AI model. The inflexible application of these rules can increase the risk that AI tools become latent in promoting, strengthening, or permitting current incidents, classify AI tools as unjustified, and diminish the level of protection for clients or the public. As a widely shared opinion influenced by numerous studies and reports, it increases inappropriate regulation, barriers to innovation, and the extension of quality legal services to a large number of potential clients, thus reducing access to justice. This has been identified as a priority opportunity for innovation and one of the main barriers to ensuring the good and widespread impacts of AI tools.

In this sense, the same study indicates the significant influence of these regulations on the orientation or development of AI tools, so it is to be expected that the rules impose quantitative limitations or qualitative restrictions on collaboration between law firms. Such as allowing the analysis of contracts, due diligence, legal investigation, or creating recipes based on the taste of the client and dinner time, but it is difficult to do so in advice development activities that require a contextual analysis that deepens and builds an enveloping environment. Restrictions on legal reliability may necessitate the creation of dynamic tools that address new realities, rules, or work through levels.

5. Future Trends and Emerging Technologies

Some of these tools and applications are used in artificial intelligence systems that we retroactively consider as things that a lawyer does or things a lawyer could do using the skills the lawyer should have. However, people who are concerned about the ethical obligations of knowledge workers, such as lawyers, have had those same concerns about the activities of healthcare workers, such as physicians. We rarely inquire when chemotherapies are used to treat tumors or when antibiotics are used to treat a bacterial infection whether the doctor is using his or her skills. If anything, we hold doctors and providers to a more stringent level of activities, higher skill levels, and greater responsibility when the usage of technologies is greater. That is the purpose of this exploration – to consider new, better, or different skills, or ways that these tools can help lawyers assist their clients better. Artificial intelligence has reached a point in its development that it is poised to ignite a future that is not yet written. It is the aim to provide only the most salient and up-to-date review of where we are now and where we are likely heading next. Though technologies are evolving, not every evolutionary stage becomes 'the next big thing.' Furthermore, assessing the adoption of new technologies is a multifaceted affair and depends on economic, social, and organizational factors as well.

5.1. Advancements in Natural Language Processing

Transformers have become the go-to building block for tackling a variety of complex language tasks and have proven to be highly effective in developing NLP models that can provide human-level quality. The idea of simply stacking the proposed transformer module repeatedly and training it in an end-to-end fashion with a language model objective has paved the way for approaches that combine predictive power and the capability of understanding human language across a number of tasks such as text classification, translation, summarization, coreference resolution, sentiment analysis, and question answering, to name a few. Excitingly, transformer-based embeddings have also been applied to a number of long-standing legal problems such as citation recommendation and text similarity scoring. Furthermore, the same transformer-based architecture is at the heart of state-of-the-art approaches to open-domain question answering tasks and has led to the development of models such as BERT, GPT, T5, and RoBERTa.

What sets transformers apart is their ability to generate rich, context-specific word representations that exploit the surrounding words to obtain a more sophisticated embedding. This has facilitated their success in applications such as these. With tens of layers and hundreds of attention heads, transformers also generate high-dimensional embeddings that pack much more information about each word. This property has been shown to be useful, particularly in transferring knowledge from pre-trained models to domain-specific NLP tasks. It is claimed that the models work so well across tasks because the underlying parameters capture a generalized understanding of human language, allowing them to transfer well to new problems without forgetting the old ones. More importantly, with a large pre-trained language model that generalizes well to unseen tasks, the fine-tuning process, which involves a large amount of labeled query information, becomes rather painless, especially compared to the effort that goes into gathering and annotating the necessary training data in the early stages of supervised learning-based NLP models.

5.2. Explainable AI and Ethical AI Design

To address the black box problem, the AI community has recently been focusing on more transparency about AI system outputs. Modern AI and ML models, especially deep models, are often criticized because the output is not transparent. These models construct the input-output relations through complicated functions. The relations between input and output are not directly observable. This often prevents AI applications from being understood and trusted by the stakeholders. However, understanding and trust are both critical to the successful deployment of AI applications. Explainable AI, or XAI, aims to explain the rationale behind the AI model output portions of its logic, the features or attributes used and their impacts, to users who are not experts in AI. XAI is a multidisciplinary area that aims to combine the AI and machine learning capabilities with human psychology and social science, the so-called dual expertise systems in AI frameworks. In the past several years, there has been an increasing number of research papers on XAI from the AI community. The research often focuses on either design principles or techniques for XAI systems, empirical and theoretical contributions to the evaluation of these systems, user studies to better understand the perceptions and needs of XAI system users, or understanding how the need for explanations can influence the behavior and decisions that AI systems generate. When it comes to designing ML and AI models to be trusted, it is not only the design that embodies ethical principles, but also to design models that can be interpreted and explained.

5.3. Integration of AI with Blockchain and IoT

It is not far off to witness the integration of blockchain and AI. AI can reinforce transaction security and validate blockchain data, and blockchain information storage may improve AI transparency and status. In the field of Internet of Things (IoT), the collaboration of AI and IoT aids hardware configuration, sensors, and networking in automation, as well as simplified application growth. Blockchain technology has become a widely discussed technology in numerous fields because of its distinctive traits such as decentralization, dedication, immutability, transparency, anonymity, and privacy protection. This study proposes a blockchain-supported exchange network—specifically, the blockchain and information storage levels, a smart way, and trust awareness level. By integrating AI into blockchain technology, an ecosystem formed by blockchain, AI, edge computing, and 5G will be established. Additionally, horizontal and vertical values of AI can be enlarged. The development of AI and blockchain jointly can significantly reduce storage costs. Conversely, the key drawbacks of blockchain, which include elongated storage time and inferior data storage performance, can be diminished through AI assistance, thus ensuring broader blockchain applicability.

5.4. Personalized Legal Services and Virtual Assistants

The aforementioned addressed applications, such as e-contracting, e-notaries, expert systems, legal research tools, document processing, and the like, may be categorized under personalized legal services and virtual assistant applications. These services are supplied to clients for responding to and generating legally binding e-documents such as NDAs, service quotes, SLAs, shareholders agreements, loans, and lease contracts indicating compensation and termination provisions, including outlining contract extensions. Document processing applications are supplied to clients for proofreading and generating documents that are part of a lawsuit, such as complaints, motions, and discovery. Expert systems are employed in judicial bodies, governmental organizations, corporations, and large law firms to speed up the process of addressing clients' questions. FAQ chatbots are used by legal departments or firms to address clients' queries and to anonymize such answers.

In summary, the purpose of legal tech services is to supply user-friendly and fast applications to respond to legal-related questions from clients or lawyers in minutes, and to draft and edit legal contracts, documents, letters, and research, providing considerable savings in money, time, and frustration. The impact or effectiveness of legal specialization AI applications depends on the specific conditions under which the tool is employed.

5.5. AI in Dispute Resolution and Courtroom Advocacy

At present, few AI applications can be found in the front line of dispute resolution and courtroom advocacy. Nevertheless, it is foreseeable that such applications will appear in the future. The aim of both litigants and the court in dispute resolution is to discover the legal facts related to the dispute case so that the case can be decided accordingly. To achieve this goal, the parties have employed not only the normal evidential means such as witness testimony, expert appraisal, and investigation but also modern digital technologies such as digital multimedia, electronic information systems, and tools.

Currently, AI technologies, especially human brain simulations, are developing rapidly, and how to incorporate such technologies into court trials has gradually become a common topic of concern. Dispute case violation measurement and legal-analysis-assisted legal fact discovery, inference, proposal, and compliance tools have already appeared. Also, like the evidence law in the traditional field, the evidence rules in the field of electronic data are essentially a balance between the compulsory requirements for the discovery of truth and the protective requirements of individuals related to information.

6. Conclusion and Recommendations

With the increased use of legal technology, it is clear that the legal field is continuing to adapt to advances when it comes to the computerization of the sector. Legal practice has changed significantly due to the technological advancements of the last fifteen years, making low-cost access to groundbreaking transformative technologies. Acceptance of legal technology is at an all-time high, when the legal profession is in the heart of integrating the formerly foreign legal technology at such speed. Legal technology is no longer considered the domain of the super-elite or an exclusive few. The enormous cost of the computer revolution has decreased; just twenty years earlier, technology of the same kind was accessible only to the largest corporate firms and exclusive law departments. No law firm or corporate legal department is currently operating without at least a minimum of scientific or artificial intelligence offerings, and a significant percentage of firms use data analysis and artificial intelligence. Almost all of the time, with the rise of technology businesses, the object has a different form and functionality. The pandemic was broadcasted in 2020 with the practice of individuals using software to raid and disrupt meetings, with searching individuals utilizing their phone camera to disturb social media meetings and generate havoc.

6.1. Summary of Key Findings

This study analyzes the essential AI tools for lawyers within the framework of the entire legal services chain. At a general level, the results denote that a total of 79 distinct AI tools exist, which are suitable for lawyers in general and legal professors in particular. However, only 58.2% of the results classify as AI solutions developed by a known organization, which could limit their functionality or general usefulness. The big problem lies in the fact that only 55.7% of the results are actually being used by lawyers today, as was to be expected since the legal profession enjoys specific features that are not habitual across other industries. From the analysis carried out, we can outline some more robust AI tools that prove to be indispensable for lawyers, such as e-discovery solutions, those implementing legal research services, litigation prediction, and even future prediction of legal impacts and events, expert systems, tools using data extraction and wrangling, those providing contract analysis, virtual agents, language models, intelligent assistants, text mining, file management, and digital marketing. It also categorizes these tools as commercial and non-commercial and also by their focus of operation. Consequently, the research concluded by bringing forward relevant issues that assist the debate on the challenges of applying these advanced technologies to advise lawyers and law professors, thus contributing to other stakeholders involved in the legal services chain. The study also brings forward contributions to various stakeholders in the field, demystifies the complex landscape of AI technology solutions in the context of the industry, and contributes to the debate on the leading utilization of the tools, making a proposal of tools of importance for research and development.

6.2. Practical Guidelines for Implementing AI Tools in Legal Practice

AI tools can support the work of lawyers by augmenting their skills and minimizing the execution of recurring and routine tasks. Integrating these tools into the workflow of lawyers and firms is not straightforward. Several practical guidelines can support a smooth implementation process. The considerations concern the range of tools used to solve a variety of business problems and the technologies that can be integrated into the workflow of diverse groups of people within the firm. The user interface and ease of use can be decisive factors for the successful uptake of AI tools. The decision-making process for integrating, buying, developing, or contracting tools is essential for an efficient use of resources. The vetting model and the training of employees are fundamental for reducing the probability of bias in AI tools and for minimizing their negative impact on decision-making processes.

Legaltech tools can improve the efficiency of existing business processes in law firms but can also make several new and non-existing processes possible. For this to happen, some steps are necessary: understanding the manual steps of traditional processes; examining a range of tools that can help complete these steps inclusively; examining the services and platforms existing to address the problems that arise; and adapting certain existing business processes to incorporate these new tools. This involves not just the decision-makers at the firm but all associated staff and, most importantly, the clients. Only this way can we generate and design new business processes and operations with AI-inspired tools in mind, making better allocation of present and new resources.

CHAPTER 7: EXPLORING FUTURE TRENDS IN LEGAL TECHNOLOGY: WHAT TO EXPECT FOR THE LEGAL PROFESSION IN THE AGE OF AI

1. Future Trends and Innovations in Legal Technology

As more AI legal technology solutions appear and as AI trails behind human-level abilities in categorization and natural language processing, next-stage tools and platforms, including legal analytics, edge closer to competence to replace today's common types of knowledge worker tasks in the labor market. However, the prospects of large-scale labor market dislocations are even broader than traditionally conceived in that a variety of new jobs such as labeling litigation documents and developing machine learning applications are originally considered tasks more suitable for a human to perform rather than a machine. Furthermore, traditional human tasks might remain relevant for a much longer term than is generally believed today due to realism and other factors significant in many legal situations. With increasing human-AI complementarities in production mix, hardware, software, and data expertise distribution, and social and economic incentives, labor-complementary AI strategies, in addition to human-capital investment strategies, can potentially alleviate some of the negative effects of AI adversity.

Law offers a fantastic area in which to explore some of the factors leading to today's "AI effect" through two different yet interconnected special features. Firstly, most legal disputes essentially dispute one of some physical or virtual rights governed by the law from the point of jurisdiction. Legal rules in a jurisdiction are a localized window of jurisdictional activity, and AI systems perform well in a data-rich environment. Compared with routine-based AI research and mainstream big data business, legal tasks concerning jurisdiction might benefit from being harder to decompose, such as some of the responsiveness provided. Secondly, filling in one of those well-established "solution matrices" involves a host of factors that are external to the AI system per se, for example, important secondary questions such as timing, costs, enforceability, or solution-matching risk. Often there is a counterparty who can disturb the solution, or the court extends new ratios or distinguishing criteria from the recurrence of similar fact situations. Balancing the nature of legal reasoning, substantial model abuse, and partial leverage levels modulates the extent of disruptive AI on the manpower and profitability of some functions in the workflow.

1.1. Predictive Analytics and Decision Support Systems

Predictive analytics has the potential to revolutionize legal practice by improving legal operations, including marketing, and by better performing substantive legal tasks such as predictive analytics, document analytics, and computer vision, among others. Predictive analytics identifies meaningful patterns in data using historical and other business and domain knowledge, and then applies those patterns to new data to predict the outcomes of future cases or inform business decision-making. Legal analytics tools can improve litigation success by forecasting case outcomes, utilizing legal research and brief-drafting tools, and selecting effective legal procedures. Similarly, prediction models help law firms better understand the market and legal needs and offer more tailored services through segmentation and marketing. In-house legal teams also use legal analytics to understand litigation risk, forecast legal spending, and inform business strategies. Predictive tools estimate the cost of discovery and review. Similarly, document analysis tools can cull and label documents and collaborate with other technology, such as contract management.

AI, including predictive analytics, is also used as an expertise engine to improve legal decision-making. Rather than replacing them, these systems provide decision support as well as precision to better meet the growing needs and expectations of legal decision-makers. Innovative legal applications can be combined with a large amount of open data and the knowledge of experts to deliver more accurate predictions for court decisions, legal precedents, and the legal status of natural persons and legal entities, among other issues. Post-segregation filtering and document labeling tools also help legal professionals in other use cases, such as due diligence exercises and investigations or contract management. Thanks to post-segregation filtering tools, contract managers and legal professionals can better detect critical clauses. Legal AI combines deep learning models, active learning strategies, and a specific iterative process to immediately inform contract managers of a risk through a web interface that indicates how to identify clauses and assess risks.

1.2. Natural Language Processing and Contract Analysis

Natural Language Processing (NLP) can support complex AI decision-making systems that accurately emulate human capabilities in areas such as understanding and summarizing documents, conversations, speech, and recommendations of actions. It can do this at scale. State-of-the-art algorithms for machine reading and understanding natural language surpass performance for specific comprehension questions posed by humans. Pretrained large language models have significantly reduced the need to hand-engineer a range of natural language processing systems. These artificial intelligence systems have become increasingly democratized and accessible.

In the legal space, there have been numerous successful commercial forays. These range from systems that review documents, contract lifecycle management, contract risk assessment, content and knowledge management, litigation prediction, legal research, know your client, compliance automation, identifying sensitive information, deal support, trademark monitoring, and company case management systems. It has been indicated that "a shift is underway to replace lawyers with computers" and that technology will improve the quality and delivery of legal services by engaging in advanced data manipulation, machine learning, agent programs, and better natural language interfaces. This prediction has not significantly materialized.

2. Education and Training for Legal Professionals in the AI Era

The education and training of the legal professionals of the future are important, and practitioners and regulators need to adapt to the changes that technology may bring. Continuous professional development of those working in the law is the best way to meet the rapidly evolving changes that technology may bring. Approximately 40% of the tasks that are currently performed by solicitors could be automated. Those entering the profession need to be equipped with the right skills to be able to make the best use of technologies such as AI. There is an increasing range of further and higher education courses available that contain law and technology-based content. To understand AI and how it affects the potential shaping of the legal environment, this content needs to be studied across a range of academic disciplines.

Technologists need to understand the legal and regulatory environment to ensure that systems that are developed are capable of working within the legal framework of society. Unless algorithms and models are developed by considering the constraints of the legal framework in a transparent and explainable manner, it will not be possible to justify the preferred actions and decisions they produce. Regulators of AI systems need to understand how AI is being used in their regulated sectors to be able to provide appropriate oversight. Lawyers and others working in the legal systems will increasingly need a working knowledge of what AI does and how AI operates to be able to participate in regulating this increasingly influential technology. This would help define auditing and certification requirements needed to have assurance in AI systems for regulators and users alike.

2.1. Skills and Competencies Required

Several skill sets and competencies are crucial to success in this new age of AI and legal services. The most important skill in the upcoming legal world will be "technology literacy," by which is meant "an appreciation of what can be achieved with the inventive use of technology, ideally coupled with an understanding of what may be achieved." This includes an understanding of the capabilities and limitations of technology and the ability to translate that understanding into effective client service and business value. One will need to develop a wide range of abilities to navigate successfully in the digital world. More generally, to be successful in law firms, courts, and legal departments of the future, one will need to be a legal doctor, client developer, business director, process improvement adviser, project manager, technologist, and above all, a continuous learner. Above all, the success and survival of the market and personal happiness must be reinvented by the traditional agent of legal advice: the legal professional. The reinvention we must envision demands new skills and the use of disruptive tools.

2.2. Integration of Legal Tech in Curricula

Technological advancements started to be more prominently included in law curricula in the early 2000s. At that time, there was also a relation with the new challenges raised for the international and regional bar exams, comprehending questions that evaluate professional ethical behavior in a technological and global legal environment. Reviewing the insertion of technology in law programs surveys legal tech modules available in countries with relevant global importance: United States, United Kingdom, European Union, India, China, Russia, Middle East, and Latin America. Those countries are considered to be the most relevant mostly because of their collective importance, therefore making it easier to understand future patterns of technological knowledge in the law field applied to different jurisdictions that are ethnically and culturally diverse. The listed countries match the main spots on global university rankings and on the top 50 rankings of legal education institutions.

3. The Future of Legal Services: Disruption and Transformation

The legal services status quo is now under the threat of disruption from a variety of actors willing to take advantage of the benefits afforded by new technologies. It is quite possible that the changes witnessed in the legal industry over the next decade will be unlike any previously observed. This general thesis has now been repeated to the point of triteness, although with a less significant immediate impact than initially thought. After a prolonged period of low-tech stagnation, legal services are now one of the focal points for technological change, with a variety of technologies and delivery mechanisms emerging.

This technological change is a reflection of the demand for affordable, efficient, reliable, transparent, and flexible legal services. Users of legal services are no longer willing to absorb the cost of inefficiency, archetype, and costliness that legal professionals sometimes impose. Indeed, surveys show that a significant portion of the public forgo legal representation, or the use of courts entirely, as they do not consider access to legal services affordable or efficient. It is now possible to access online forms for drafting routine legal documents, innovative advice and representation firms of different sizes, legal managed services, third-party litigation funders, regulatory lawtech platforms, advocacy chatbots, alternative dispute resolution mechanisms, predictive analysis of court cases, and marketplaces of legal services and funding using third-party investment.

3.1. *Emerging Business Models in Legal Services*

A notable consequence of new technologies, particularly AI, in the legal services space, is the emergence of new service models. A key driver of this change is a movement from product-oriented services to value-based billings. Clients are increasingly seeking the services of law firms that will deliver practical and bespoke solutions to their legal issues. Firms that offer a strict and formulaic 'product' are less likely to attract profitable legal work. This shift has seen a large number of mid-tier accounting and law firms aggressively attempt to wrestle market share from traditional premium legal service providers. The immediate question arises – who then can offer the best value for money in legal services? How are the traditional professors of the law reacting to what is happening all around them? Where are they investing their money in order to stay competitive? What is true irrespective of the law firm model is that client expectations are driving a need for increased cost efficiency. A heavy reliance on expensive human resources is therefore hard to sustain in legal services, complemented by an increase in operational and financial risk. The use of technology in providing legal services ranges from simple automations that cause a revolution to new service models. These heavily involve AI, where approval of information anywhere in the work value chain is not required. What we are saying is more than mere speculation – these evolutionary and even revolutionary processes are now well underway.

3.2. *Impact on Access to Justice*

First and foremost, the impact of legal technology is likely to be significant in improving access to justice. This is already making headway, with technology now being widely used not only to provide access to justice for those who have no access to lawyers but also to streamline dispute resolution infrastructure. There is now a plethora of online dispute resolution platforms available that assist consumers at all levels in their disputes. These institutions enable visitors to solve the most simple legal questions without persuading them to visit an attorney, offering them both legal aid and representation in court. Technologies and programs deployed in this field would be crucial in enhancing the legal protection of ordinary users who may have difficulties accessing lawyers or other resources. In addition, many developed nations have invested in digitization and in creating the institutions that can use that. In this context, it is possible to believe that legal technology can help repair or at least alleviate current systemic malfunctions. Making less expensive schemes work in the United States, where the power of a widely growing and partially unregulated legal profession stands at stake in these conversations, could create potential models for the United States. Preliminary success has already been established in serving the marginalized in some foreign jurisdictions and particular areas where government-directed unified legal professions are less popular than in the U.S. Interestingly, legal technology appears to be a continuous field for improvements in access to justice, for better or worse, under a range of global jurisprudential systems.

4. Collaboration between Lawyers and Technologists

Emerging technologies such as AI can only be fully harnessed by fostering interdisciplinary groups that combine both legal and computer engineering skills. As for the legal community, its professional practice should stimulate and empower interdisciplinary collaboration among legal experts and computer software engineers. The communication gap between the professional practice of law and the science and technologies that support it still reveals a lack of understanding of the potential and limitations of justice done by machines in contemporary environments of digital legal challenges. No longer an option, interdisciplinary dialogue and recruitment in computer profiles are required for an adequate understanding and development of future trends. The avenue of formal education and specialized training of domain specialists with a clear knowledge of the current state of science and technology and how to use it wisely in the designed intelligent systems is essential. At the same time that you design with science and technology based on law, the computational and informative deductions about law are used for the implementation of legal models in the new programming models of a new society that makes use of digital and intelligent agents to access its legal order. Therefore, the synergy between law and computational sciences and technologies is decisive. The urgency for graduation and post-graduation programs aimed at the interdisciplinarity of law along with STEM is an open door to recognition and respect.

4.1. Interdisciplinary Teams in Legal Tech Development

Machine learning models perform tasks as well as human beings and are now one of the most revolutionary technologies ever. The use of ML models and AI technologies in law has created new responsibilities and professional risks for both attorneys and judges. These high-stakes responsibilities have pushed the legal community to meet novel challenges, and achieving this has required the work of not just smart lawyers and judges, but also technology experts. This change in the legal community goes beyond coding bootcamps. Rather, it increasingly requires the creation of interdisciplinary teams that work across various organizational areas, multiple law and policy disciplines, courts, police departments, executive agencies, civil society, and more. As a result, the gaping division between those trained in the law and those who are studying technology has finally become an area of focus in the background of legal education.

While current legal tech studies are producing promising outcomes, most of the research on legal applications of machine learning and AI still comes from computer science and engineering departments. Consequently, the evidence base is still emerging, and leading law scholars have created expert lists in an effort to bolster visibility and increase joint work. Most of the interdisciplinary work to date has been between law and ethics or law and economics, but as legal tech burgeons, this is expected also to burgeon. Surely, future legal learnings will be much more inter- and multi-disciplinary than in the past. Universities and law firms have certainly taken notice and launched joint efforts to bring these types of thinkers together, usually under the moniker of 'legal tech institutes' or 'innovation, technology, and entrepreneurship' programs that overlap with scholarly writing and coding bootcamps. The going is slow, but law's shift into the interdisciplinary direction is now very much upon us.

4.2. Effective Communication and Collaboration

Clients often feel left in the dark with no access to the information showing progression on their case. Lawyers also often spend a lot of time on the phone or in meetings with clients, updating them about the status of their case. Collaboration and client communication tools will increase and improve client engagement and the attorney-client relationship. Both of these tools are making strides in creating opportunities, phases, and tasks to work closely with clients. These tools will expand as they connect more and more with other technologies, such as updating a legal matter and producing the requested documents as evidence in a trial. At first, clients will be happy to receive regular feedback. This will give them peace of mind, result in faster turnaround times, and allow attorneys to take on more clients. Second, clients will begin to expect regular updates. These tools will then most probably change from being a competitive differentiator to becoming a must-have or even a standard requirement for clients to connect with a law firm. Third, clients will most probably become more involved throughout the process as they become more comfortable with receiving regular feedback. They will be better informed and also understand the attorney's processes and service delivery.

5. Challenges and Barriers to Adoption of Legal Tech

Judicial and legal reforms that take account of accelerated technological change require skills and expertise that the judiciary and the legal profession are, for the most part, not currently well-equipped to provide. However, legal professionals remain subject to the fundamental principle codified in the task to deliver justice. As machine learning technology becomes increasingly important in supporting decision-making in the legal process, the public interest demands that legal professionals be cognizant of key issues related to AI and the responsibilities that arise for the professional community as a result. Every challenge can be seen as an opportunity. The characteristics of AI that recent technological progress illuminate likely facilitate an AI-assisted system for better judgment and prevent biases. Despite these positive implications, attorneys and judges are slow to adopt legal tech using AI models in the key processes. There are various discussions about challenges to deploying AI tools in these key processes. This special issue aims to explore these challenges and, by doing so, lists the following four critical themes—AI unexplainability, liability, transparency, and enhancement in the protection of human rights. These four themes are particularly significant from the perspective of achieving a practical deployment. Online-mediated dispute resolution has already begun; however, we should keep striving to realize these opportunities, keeping in mind these four challenges.

5.1. Cost and Return on Investment

As attorneys are increasingly pressured to conduct efficient legal work, legal technology should strive to provide attorneys with the data necessary to make the most efficient decisions. This data will not only need to provide information about potential cost fluctuations in the middle of a legal battle, but also make it easier to understand how technology itself may wrap up legal matters quicker. When this technology is able to be used by clients in real time, they may in turn seek to use only the attorney who can actually prove the ability to have a reasonable return on investment. Additionally, all attorneys that cater to businesses are aware of the fact that if you increase business risk (or the cost to do business), the competitive entities will not just hang around and let the market fall into a pit without a fight. AI technology should help to make legal assistance more affordable and bring about a more general legal culture. This is not to be put aside as impractical navel-gazing, but will likely occur as larger legal corporations will do what they can to get rich or die trying. The future legal tiers may even hunger for the least bit of unattended need or want.

5.2. Resistance to Change in the Legal Profession

The legal profession, like other professions, is not immune to the Luddite fallacy—the false assumption that a new technology would destroy jobs. New technology does not displace any meaningful proportion of lawyers, but it empowers them to work more efficiently and pursue complex problems more imaginatively. We will always require large teams of highly talented attorneys to resolve highly complex legal disputes. The only difference is that future teams of talented lawyers will be empowered by advances in AI and legal technology to do far more, far more quickly. Once relief from inefficient drudgery becomes a right, it immediately creates other new, more meaningful and satisfying work. Quality and scale are no longer trade-offs to manage, and the driving legal technology will actually become a significant enabler of good—providing greater access to justice, improving the quality of justice, and expanding the role played by the ombudsman of the law.

6. Global Perspectives on Legal Tech Adoption

Unique domestic political and economic market conditions also affect the pace and intensity at which countries have adopted a growing array of legal technology offerings, which in the AI era include an even more global range of companies marketing AI legal analytics tools and products. From an early stage, some countries embraced legal technology, while others were more tepid in their enthusiasm, aided by larger home markets and sometimes government support or even formal action plans. Other factors affect when and how legal technology is adopted and employed. The relative power of corporate counsel versus law firms and its possible impact on law department hiring and deployment of legal technology varies by country. Decisions on whether and how to deploy technology, especially in lower margin segments, are also sensitive to the opportunity cost embedded in financial investment and the time to gain work experience and critical legacy lawyers skills that can be essential later in life.

The review of the relative size of country legal sectors as an aggregate of law firms, corporate law departments, and in-house governmental units showed sharp disparities that are to an extent driven by the size of country GDPs. For comparative purposes, we employed a definitional threshold of $10,000 per capita per year for each category. The countries in the $10,000 – $15,000 per year categories are Turkey at $11,155 and Tunisia at $11,522, followed by Mexico, South Africa, and Greece. At the high end, the countries with per capita incomes of greater than $40,000 range from France and Portugal, which lie below $45,000 per week, to Norway, the Netherlands, Denmark, Canada, Germany, Switzerland, and the UK, which perch comfortably between $45,000 and $65,000. Each of these Western European countries not surprisingly harbors extensive and active legal sectors, though with very different balances between private and in-house practice.

6.1. Regional Differences in Legal Tech Uptake

That last section leads nicely to the topic of regional differences in the uptake of legal technology. I believe that differences such as those related to economic development, access to legal services, bar regulatory systems, and the governmental underpinnings of legal systems are relevant; their impact on ILTA members in the United States may influence the global trajectory of 21st-century lawyering. This conference has engaged a robust contingent from the Asia-Pacific region, and valuable perspectives have been shared by participants from Europe as well. Characteristics of the Western traditions in which ILTA largely operates can be taken for granted by proponents of legal technology, but they provide powerful evidence of how legal professionalism and legal services are conducted. They may point the way for 21st-century lawyering.

The contrast of private bar and state court culture with those of other countries offers some insight into the dynamics of a highly mature national legal tech toolbox and trend analysis; that is, that of the US. Its immigration, languages, ethnicities, and income disparities shape its disputes, judicial norms, and roles in a manner that other countries lack. The United States legal profession is also governed by specific client conflicts of interest rules that make it less relatable to its European and Asia-Pacific counterparts. The widespread, albeit disparate, regulation of legal services delivery through such entities as US state supreme courts and state bars ensures that rule-making remains fragmented, removed from the controversies of the moment, and reflects not current social needs, but past norms.

6.2. International Standards and Regulations

Challenges lie not only in the technical development of these technologies, but also in setting the guidelines for their use to mitigate security risks, as well as economic and social issues. The discussion on what guidelines should be taken is a topic on developing independent standards for ensuring the trustworthiness of these technologies and stimulating their uptake. This is a cross-cutting issue that is not only relevant for research, but also for standardization development and legal aspects. Appropriate standards for ethics and data governance for AI and data technologies need to be developed based on international legal frameworks and principles, which then need to be effectively implemented through policies and regulations.

The incentives behind some existing conventions or international law targeting automation using AI or big data have existed for a range of years. Ethical principles require states to respect ethical principles in case the decision to use force is delegated to an autonomous weapon; the best interest is a primary consideration in decisions regarding children; data processing must respect fundamental rights and properly use technical and organizational restrictions to guarantee the security of the processed data. However, these are not directly binding, lack clarity, and are neither well-defined nor measurable values of ethics or data governance, nor universally acceptable ethical principles, nor defined measures to guarantee the principles through technical means. The regulatory mechanisms have yet to adapt and evolve to support guidelines to be implemented and enforced. This issue is particularly salient in an era of geopolitics, and given the immense diversity with regard to legal, regulatory, technological, and political cultures around the world, the development of global regulatory frameworks is a complex and pressing challenge that will require coordination and alignment among not just policymakers, but also academia and industry.

7. The Role of Government and Policy in Shaping Legal Tech

Government plays a critical role in the creation and protection of a free market that supports innovation and competition in the legal service market. Regulation must balance the needs of consumers with the risk of regulating the technology and solutions out of existence. Government interests in the field of legal technology include the ability to develop a competitive legal service industry that can assist in the protection and proper integration of new technology, as well as facilitate competition among companies that provide different services and operate at different scales. There is also a significant role for government in the delivery of public access to the legal system.

The private sector and government have different objectives in developing and deploying technology, and these objectives must be balanced if the great benefits of America's multilayered system of law and regulation are to be realized. The private sector must develop its technology to provide a profit, and while the presence of competition generally drives improvements in quality and application, these advances are aimed at finding the specific segments where marketing success is profitable. By comparison, government programs are in place to support the overall mission of the state, in the areas of law enforcement, the military, and other government functions. Differences in these objectives also lead to different incentives and constraints that must be recognized when developing relevant technologies. For governments to maximize the benefits of major technological advances, they need to be proactive supporters, participants, and funding sources for research and development. Governments should also be active supporters of key standards and encourage close cooperation between research laboratories and private industry, consulting, and service companies.

7.1. Government Initiatives and Funding

Several countries are investing significantly in the development of AI technologies with a view to making more money now and in the future. The European Commission is pooling its resources to create a European initiative on artificial intelligence, funding projects among EU member states to the tune of €20 billion, with €1.5 billion of this amount coming from the European Commission and other partners. The participants aim to seek out solutions and establish research lines and strategies. This funding is aimed at supporting both the research and the development of technological solutions based on AI and its use. In Canada, the federal and provincial governments have recently announced initiatives to support AI. In the case of the US, while the previous administration has not announced any investment programs, the US accounts for the highest proportion of global AI investment. The Chinese government has made artificial intelligence a strategic priority and has stated that its goal is to become a world leader in AI by 2030.

Funding is a necessary prerequisite to achieving these ambitious objectives in the area of AI. The idea behind governments investing in AI is all about making as much money as possible and reaching these goals quickly. AI could put the government a few steps ahead and save time in many areas. For example, rather than checking real estate records with the city hall, people could instead ask a legal AI about prior occupancy rights, the possible impacts of an easement, or what a particular law stipulates. These are all time-consuming tasks that AI could simplify, making information easy to find. This argument applies to both access to information and administrative processes. In addition, people generally associate the work of public-sector employees with essential and reliable information. With the resources of the government of Canada, people would therefore be that much more confident in finding reliable and relevant answers. If used effectively, it is a win-win situation for both the public and private sectors.

7.2. Policy Implications of AI in Law

Policymakers and society at large need to consider the far-reaching impacts AI will have on law and the legal profession. Potentially exacerbating existing challenges or creating new issues, the impact of AI in law could have direct and indirect effects on numerous domains of law, legal systems, and the administration of justice. We must begin planning for these policy implications, or we risk the unintended consequences that could result. This chapter reviews several of the future policy implications and challenges AI in law presents to the legal community and identifies some not particularly controversial but important questions that we will have to grapple with.

Will AI in law create greater systemic bias? AI systems learn from data; thus, if large data samples are negatively biased, such as arrest statistics reflecting biased police activity, then it is reasonable to assume that AI trained on such data may also exhibit those biases. This systemic bias has already been explored in the context of facial recognition data. If AI in law systems learn from biased data, jurisdictions utilizing these systems may end up with more accurate biased systems. The impact on systemic bias of courts and prosecutors from using machine learning tools is a conversation society as a whole now needs to consider.

8. The Intersection of Legal Tech with Other Fields

Introduction. In this book, I have predominantly discussed a number of future trends in legal tech. These trends are relevant to the technology, the LPP, and the other fields that law intersects with. In this regard, one trend should have become obvious to the reader from the very beginning: even though the focus of this paper has been legal technology, the considerations are meant to apply to law and any other field. Post-After Word hence looks at the ways that legal tech might intersect with other fields in the future, even past the point of becoming 'legal' tech anymore.

Intersecting with the technological future of other fields. The main focus of the first seven trends explored the ways in which technological transformations will change the role of legal professionals. However, technological changes will, of course, also transform the work of people in other areas. There are countless other discussions about what the various fields that intersect with law need to understand about the technology of their own future, but here are some cross-cutting observations we can make across multiple fields, inspired by each of the seven previous trends.

8.1. Legal Tech in Healthcare and Insurance

Without a doubt, no other area in future trends in legal technology has so much potential awaiting as healthcare and insurance. This is because both areas have highly structured data that can be mapped, analyzed, and mined, providing a unique intersection of the legal with the economic and statistical sciences and requiring a very large and growing body of rules with high levels of certainty. In the developed world, constantly pressured healthcare systems could avoid several unnecessary liabilities, medical errors, and their corresponding costs by applying the predictive capabilities of artificial intelligence. Cases of medical malpractice, which consume a large portion of healthcare budgets and human lives, could be largely curbed by early detection of high-risk doctors or hospitals, or more generally of low-quality or abusive practices, or incidents that could lead to compensation rights violations. The largest relative increase in AI use is expected in insurance companies, which use big data algorithms to capitalize on the insights of IoT devices and big data. Insurance companies are increasingly being digitally enabled for customer, underwriting, and operational insights, delivering a differentiated and personalized customer experience in real time. Services in this area can include improved cross-channel customer service through faster claim resolution, risk assessment through predictive modelling and price optimization, process improvement, remote diagnostics and maintenance, outsourcing of non-core activities, fraud detection, and exposure risk reduction, among others. The impurification of almost everything, from cars, homes, and the internet to health and life risks, will further drive industry innovation and collaboration – namely through the use of telematics, peer-to-peer indemnity, pay-per-mile, pay-as-you-live, and group benefit programs.

8.2. Cross-Industry Collaboration Opportunities

Cross Industry Opportunities: With AI and machine learning capabilities exceeding the grasp of most single industries, there is ample opportunity for cross-industry collaboration, including among those organizations generally perceived as competitors. Within the legal domain alone, we anticipate that legal commentators, governments, the judiciary, regulators, and bar associations will work more cooperatively to meet common objectives that support a robust and thoughtful use of AI in legal practice. Key tasks to address are ensuring effective data partnerships and proper regulatory sandboxes for AI projects; pushing for algorithms that result in accurately congruent results in ranking cases to ensure effective judicial decision-making; ensuring that the requirements and ethical implications are understood by all legal professionals, and that there are guidelines to support their usage; ensuring standard practices and support around how required security and client confidentiality elements can be managed; and pushing for transparency and comfort that the final decision made by the machine is both justifiable and understandable.

9. The Future of Legal Tech Startups and Innovation

Every year, analysts, experts, lawyers, legal professionals, technologists, and even a growing number of the general public look to the yearly conference on legal tech in New York. One of the truisms of this conference is that the arena of legal tech is always changing and always developing. Legal tech and companies that engage in legal tech are evolving and moving, and every year there is a growth in the number of companies in that arena. The growing intervention of artificial intelligence in today's legal practice will also prompt many new companies to take a space at next year's conference.

From an assessment of the rate of change and growth observable at the conference, legal tech resembles something of a gold rush. Numerous startups are trying to commercialize the intersection between law and technology. As a practitioner fingers through piles of tickets from vendors seeking yet another large startup prize, carefully observing breaks and hostess gifts, he might wonder where all those vendors are really going. Where in legal technology is the gold seam found? Which legal tech categories offer the potential for continued growth, and which may be a bored hole in the ground? The following are predictions on categories that are beginning to show activity—trends that indicate areas where future growth will likely be.

9.1. Incubators and Accelerators in Legal Tech

Incubators and accelerators in legal tech are set to stay, with over 70% of survey firms expecting the number to grow over the next five years. The set have one key expectation of these organizations, which is to get early-stage start-ups that they can nurture, which would be very difficult to do in-house or outsource. While some of the lawyers in the survey believe that the services these organizations provide will be moved in-house, they expect their numbers to decrease because they are new and currently growing. However, 70% of the surveyed organizations have never provided funding to a legal tech company, making us wonder how much their expectations are grounded in reality and not hope.

The predominantly sole founders of legal tech companies were typically professionals with technical skills such as programming, designing, and research, supplied by legal professionals such as lawyers, judges in the criminal and civil sense, IT managers, paralegals, and contract managers respectively. Surprisingly, law students and recent graduates were very few and far between. For the products, over 70% catered to business persons, while over 30% catered to the public in the form of public interest, access to justice, and non-profit company interactions. The most attention from the survey organizations can be summarized as being new and cool, with a noticeable trend said to result from the increasing commodification of law. Why one would want to shape strategy around something new and cool versus something in demand is hard to understand.

9.2. Investment Trends in Legal Tech

There are three prominent trends that are developing in the legal sector when it comes to investments in legal tech solutions. The first trend involves the diversification of investments in the legal tech market. The legal tech ecosystem is developing steadily, with a growing number of providers offering specialized solutions for law firms and in-house legal departments. As the already crowded legal tech market continues to grow in scale and complexity, the need to strategically structure investments in this space becomes even more important. This includes understanding which legal tech start-ups are getting the lion's share of venture capital investments, what solutions are receiving the most attention from legal departments, what the current range of investor motivations might be, and what potential opportunities and challenges are associated with each of these different factors.

Secondly, the legal profession is also a field that is positively adaptive to embracing innovative and new technologies. For example, blockchain technology is being hailed as the upcoming Internet with a unique capability to revolutionize every industry, including legal. Immutable blockchain data could be utilized as evidence in legal disputes. Smart contracts, which are self-executing contracts, will streamline legal service efficiency by encoding their own contracts on blockchain and thereby removing the intermediaries. AI and robo-advisors will formulate and serve legal documents, offer legal advisory, predictions, research, and manage data that will require attorneys to evolve and offer more personalized value-added human elements. Many governmental organizations, public and private companies, attorneys, and the larger public are all actively exploring and funding blockchain technology and applications. However, these forward-looking innovations require various pre-approvals, including legal audits, at either pre-implementation or post-adaptive stages from legal and accounting perspectives. At the same time, legal advisors will serve as advisors and educators for stakeholders, as well as pace officers to uphold and enforce these new creations.

CHAPTER 8: THE FUTURE LAWYER: ADAPTING WITH PURPOSE, LEADING WITH COURAGE

1. The Legal Profession at a Crossroads

The Legal Profession is at a Crossroads. And it is not alone. There is much talk of a "Great Resignation." The COVID Pandemic, the shock of the Black Lives Matter Movement, and years of work-life unbalance in the 24/7 news cycle of social media have so fatigued and disillusioned workers young and not so young that many have left higher paying jobs for identify-affirming jobs that align more closely with their personal values. Tens of thousands of lawyers across the globe are clamouring for more flexibility and a better "work to life" ratio that satisfies their quest for purpose, fulfilment, autonomy, and balance. More than ever before, they are willing to take a pay cut and transition out of Big Law and Healthcare Corporate Law and the high legal fees of law firms dominating M&A and ECM, instead transitioning into solo and small firm practice dedicated to social justice priorities or work for a nonprofit or government agency that has an important role in hiring a much larger number of lawyers from diverse backgrounds.

Economic demand is depressed in some if not many legal practice areas like securities, mergers and acquisitions, and areas of complex corporate and commercial matters at the very same time that innovation in AI is transforming the legal landscape, making the delivery of routine legal services by many lawyers at wage rates much lower than they currently charge impractical if not impossible. Demand is returning in others such as real estate, estate planning, and family law, but these areas do not pay the large salaries associated with the traditionally cushy jobs of lawyers in Big Corporate Law Firms. The estimated that AI and Fourth Industrial Revolution innovations combined will displace 75 million jobs, many in the office-clerical sector. But 97 million new jobs will be created in the new economy.

2. What AI Can and Cannot Do

Just as the advent of computers shifted the role of lawyers from creating and validating documents to interpreting and applying the law, so too will AI further automate specific tasks of legal practitioners. So, lawyers will remain engaged in tasks that computers cannot perform such as human interactions with clients, opposing parties, judges, and juries. In their dealings with clients, lawyers must ensure that their representations are made and received along the lines of established legal ethics. It is precisely in these areas of human interactions based on interpersonal relationships, empathy, and ethical considerations, where humans will always have an advantage over AI.

The introduction of any new technology invariably leads to the successful completion of tasks previously performed under the supervision and oversight of humans by the new technology. Human involvement in the tasks, however, will not disappear. Search engines, for example, are capable of crawling the globe's online information without assistance. Still, they require humans to develop their algorithms, ensure that their results are timely and maximally relevant, and fill the search engines with usefully tagged information. A growing industry comprised of thousands of workers exists precisely for that last function, as do companies dedicated to data management and curation.

So, too, lawyers will find that AI can streamline their work. Rather than generate casework opinions where there can be a significant volume of similar claims that allow for the creation of templates populated by AI with specifics for unique cases, AIs will become increasingly able to engage in the grunt work of document review, due diligence, and brief and contract drafting, where underlying rules can be manipulated by a computer system to create customized documents in a timely fashion. Indeed, both international accounting firms that provide legal services and large law firms have developed AI tools that do just that.

3. My Journey

My personal journey into the world of artificial intelligence began at a serendipitous moment in early 2017. I realized that law was going through a seismic shift, across every sector and every jurisdiction, primarily driven by the impact of AI on knowledge work. It was clear that lawyers were faced with a choice: to continue on the same hamstrung career path of previous generations, or to pivot and amplify their roles, using AI as a partner to advance the common good. Even though I was not formally trained in the field, I felt a fulfilment to be one of the guides showing lawyers how to adapt and succeed in this new world. I describe my place in that journey as one of a scout. I had no idea what the destination looked like; I simply went ahead exploring the new landscape, hoping that I could help others along the way. In that spirit, I invited lawyers to join me. I wrote articles about AI's impact on the legal profession, as well as newsletters and podcasts. The world was changing and I wanted to help lawyers adapt to that new reality by sharing how I discovered ground-breaking AI applications in useful business settings. Moreover, like any new civilization that flourished after the hunter-gatherers, we now also needed a new civilized infrastructure: the Law Labor Registry, which would allow lawyers to utilize all this transformative technology and get paid for it. A market somehow. Without a labor registry, that new marketplace will be chaotic and lacking credibility. That new public infrastructure can be the basis for a new model that democratizes access to legal services.

4. Lightening the Mental Load

The business of law is partly about serving clients and society – but even more it is about attracting, training, and retaining strong, empowered lawyers. And the extraordinary demands of modern legal practice, especially in a climate of increased competition and decreasing client loyalty, add a significant burden to an already overburdened profession. Women in the profession experience this burden even more acutely than their male counterparts, and lawyers who are parents, especially of young children, are being floored by the mental load of endlessly juggling the demands of home and work. For more than 30 years, research studies have shown that women, even those in two-parent families where dad is home much of the time, continue to do the vast majority of domestic work – laundry, cleaning, grocery shopping, cooking, remembering school lunches, planning kids' playdates and birthday parties, keeping track of medical and dental appointments, attending all the meetings at school, and so on.

While time at the office is often more strictly defined – opening hours, billable hours, and deadlines create a clear expectation of availability – when it comes to work hours outside the office, lawyers themselves – women especially – still feel called on to demonstrate their devotion to work by being available to client demands 24/7. And because lawyers are typically performing professional services, not producing a tangible product within a narrow window of hours, it is difficult to measure lawyer productivity. But in a profession where burnout has been shown to be symmetrical to pro-bono service – a test of individuals' belief that they are giving back to their community – there is a high correlation between employee dissatisfaction and the number of hours worked without satisfaction.

5. Humanising Law Again

Technology allowed a law business to spin outward towards clients as it controlled and streamlined its processes internally, but a law business that cannot deliver equivalent service through its frontline is going to fall behind. Law is still a service business, and human contact has to be engaged at the branding level, with all else being equal. What, then, is the brand offering? When we consider the effects of globalisation on our business, try for a moment to consider your answer to that question to be the decisions made by the partners of a leading law firm. What is going to be the offer promised to clients by the top city firms in the years of their post-graduate clearance for competition? What sensibilities or experiences will differentiate service, and why should a client sweep aside its memories of facile interaction, overstated prices, and indifferent response to simple queries, to return for what matters most: the contractual reaction between company X and company Y, when the transaction (and the advice) is at last clearly defined for mutual benefit. And at what price, or rather price differentiation, will partners risk? The answers to those questions are delicate.

The third dimension of a brand's offering is the level and quality of individual contact between staff and clients. On price, a leading law firm would appear to have an advantage. With the efficiencies that technology permits, hourly rates across the board will decline. There may also be economies of scale for the larger firms. However, more than any other service business, legal services rely on the individual lawyers who are engaged, and first impressions may decide both the future actions of clients, and whether those clients return. A global brand in lieu of a professional partner will not cut it. It need not involve intimate service at every level, but you cannot simply think in terms of providing a service.

6. A Reflection, Not a Checklist

There are no rules for what the future lawyer looks like; rather, these are thoughts for everyone in the profession to reflect on, taking their own viewpoints, career paths and aspirations into consideration, and if, out of reflection comes realization that changes or investments are needed, this is encouragement to take that leap. You may be wanting more of a road map than questions, however, and if that is the case, the roadmap I would share supports building from the top down. The least investment and lowest risk is in short, self-study commitments, perhaps with a sprinkle of networking to tap into different viewpoints; following, as interest grows in certain areas maybe pursuing more formal learning.

As the roadmap moves from self- to team-investment, coming in the form of joint studies, perhaps with an individual or two tasked with bringing things back to a larger group or groups, this teaching to learn approach is valuable for maintaining the energy of the larger group. The biggest investment then is the group or firm making the decision to invest in that area which is why it is important to collaborate at multiple levels and from different functions to determine where are the returns. Focusing on everyone's areas of interest, these are the best places to start; whilst there may be a strong interest in artificial intelligence from a portion of your team, understanding the threat and opportunities that come with employing artificial intelligence, each person should ideally then be upskilling in their respective areas using tools that improve their execution and how they work with AI.

Mentorship from leaders and passion towards the development of your team should also be taken into account; the reason you see ex lawyers pivoting to the tech world is not because they love technology more than law, it's because at a certain stage of their career, the angle they bring for one reason or another is better suited from a tech perspective.

7. Final words

All lawyers need to accept change is coming, if not already here, and consequently adapt how they work, in order to fulfill their role in a changing society. Some lawyers have already embraced opportunities presented by change and instituted changes in their practice model to address emerging client demands and expectations. The challenge for the remainder is to recognize that resistance to change is futile, in that clients will increasingly seek alternatives, whether that be in the form of technology or different resources internally or externally, to adapt to the changing business landscape that they are, along with society, operating in. Lawyers perceived as unnecessary and/or overly costly will no longer be utilized. This does not mean that lawyers will no longer have a role in the business world, only that the nature of the role will be different. Those lawyers who refuse to take positive steps to change with the times will put their career (or the careers of those in a law firm) at risk. Lawyers who lead with purpose and courage can, and should, proactively embrace opportunities presented by change. Not only to fulfill a role within the larger economy in a changing society but to adapt to changing demands of clients to have fulfilling work and a better work-life balance. Each lawyer has the capability to embrace change to enhance his/her offering to clients, and thus himself/herself, as well as to the profession. By affirmatively taking on the challenge of developing a niche area of competence, lawyers can connect and engage not only with existing clients but with new and potential clients to support their organizations' development and objectives. In doing so, those lawyers will not only reinforce the value proposition that lawyers offer to their clients but enhance the value proposition that the profession in turn offers to society.

"The future lawyer isn't the one who resists change — it's the one who transforms it into purpose, balance, and service. We are not being replaced; we are being redefined — and we get to lead that definition."

Mohamed Darwish

www.ingramcontent.com/pod-product-compliance
Lightning Source LLC
Chambersburg PA
CBHW071321230926
51849CB00002B/286
9787764772367